Xc

Wedding Speeches and Etiquette

Visit our How To website at www.howto.co.uk

At **www.howto.co.uk** you can engage in conversation with our authors – all of whom have 'been there and done that' in their specialist fields. You can get access to special offers and additional content but most importantly you will be able to engage with, and become a part of, a wide and growing community of people just like yourself.

At **www.howto.co.uk** you'll be able to talk and share tips with people who have similar interests and are facing similar challenges in their lives. People who, just like you, have the desire to change their lives for the better – be it through moving to a new country, starting a new business, growing their own vegetables, or writing a novel.

At **www.howto.co.uk** you'll find the support and encouragement you need to help make your aspirations a reality.

How To Books strives to present authentic, inspiring, practical information in their books. Now, when you buy a title from **How To Books,** you get even more than just words on a page.

Wedding Speeches and Etiquette

JOHN BOWDEN

howtobooks

Published by How To Books Ltd
Spring Hill House, Spring Hill Road,
Begbroke, Oxford OX5 1RX
Tel: (01865) 375794 Fax: (01865) 379162
info@howtobooks.co.uk
www.howtobooks.co.uk

How To Books greatly reduce the carbon footprint of their books by sourcing their typesetting
and printing in the UK.

British Library Cataloguing in Publication Data.
A catalogue record for this book is available from the British Library.

ISBN 978 1 84528 436 7

Fifth edition 2000
Reprinted 2001 (twice), 2002, 2003, 2004, 2006
Sixth edition 2008
Seventh edition 2011

Produced for How To Books by Deer Park Productions, Tavistock, Devon
Typeset by PDQ Typesetting, Newcastle-under-Lyme, Staffordshire
Printed and bound by Bell & Bain Ltd, Glasgow

NOTE: The material contained in this book is set out in good faith for general guidance and no
liability can be accepted for loss or expense incurred as a result of relying in particular
circumstances on statements made in the book. The laws and regulations are complex and liable
to change, and readers should check the current position with the relevant authorities before
making personal arrangements.

For Paula . . . forever

Contents

Preface
to the Seventh Edition

If the combined nervous energy of brides-to-be, their fathers, their grooms and best men and women were properly harnessed, it would be sufficient to create an alternative energy source that would eradicate the need for fossil fuels. And the main cause of their collective collywobbles is their speeches.

Yet, in reality, the basics of preparing and delivering a great little speech are really quite simple and straightforward. And with the help of this book, a little imagination and a sense of humour, the task can actually be fun.

Whether you feel honoured or lumbered or perhaps both to be 'saying a few words' on the Big Day, you'll find all the advice and tips you'll need to calm those nerves and to help you create a special spellbinding speech that will sparkle like vintage champagne.

We'll begin with some general thoughts about 21st-century wedding speech etiquette and on the basics of effective public speaking. Then we'll consider each of the main traditional wedding speeches – and also the more modern optional extra ones – in greater detail.

As with most things in life, the more you put in, the more you get out – and the sooner you start, the better your contribution is likely to be. And so, with no further ado, may I ask you to be upstanding and to charge your glasses. The toast is: The wedding speakers . . . may they be infused with taste, timing and tone . . . with warmth, wit and wisdom.

My Lords, Ladies and Gentlemen, I give you . . . the speeches!

John Bowden

1
Etiquette and All That

Traditionally, there are three speeches at a wedding reception. The first is made by the bride's father or guardian; the second by the bridegroom; and the third by his best man. However, this simple pattern assumes that the bride has been brought up by two parents and today over two million people in Britain haven't been.

So now it is perfectly acceptable for speeches to be made by other people as well as – or instead of – the 'big three' – perhaps by the bride's mother, by her stepdad or stepmum, by the chief bridesmaid, by the best girl, by a child of the bride or groom, by the bride and groom jointly, or by the bride herself. It all depends on the particular circumstances, backgrounds and wishes of the newlyweds.

Being introduced

Etiquette demands that every speaker should be formally introduced. This is not only a courtesy to them, but also a courtesy to their audience. Some guests may not know who all the speakers are, so it is both good manners and good sense for someone to briefly introduce each of them in turn, giving a little background information about them and their relationship to the bride and/ or the groom.

If there is to be a professional toastmaster, he or she will be pleased to read out a short and informative intro for each speaker. If there is no toastmaster, many couples automatically ask their best man to do the honours. That's fine, but it's certainly not essential. Anyone can fulfil this role. Perhaps it could be done by the bride's stepdad, if he is not going to make a speech. Or maybe a particularly self-confident family friend or relative would be willing to do the MC-ing. What matters is that a competent person should be given the responsibility for making all the official announcements and introductions and for keeping things moving on in an interesting and entertaining manner.

When the speeches are about to begin, traditionally a professional toastmaster will call for attention and silence by rapping a gavel on the table, saying something like: 'Ladies and Gentlemen, pray silence for Mr Ben Nevis who will propose a toast to Mr Sydney and Mrs Pearl Harbour.' If a friend or relative is acting as the MC, he or she could simply jingle a spoon in an empty glass, to gain attention, before introducing the first speaker. This announcement would probably be made in a less formal manner: 'Ladies and Gentlemen, please be silent as Mr Ben Nevis proposes a toast to Mr Sydney and Mrs Pearl Harbour.' It's showtime!

Before or after the meal?

Some couples decide to have the speeches before the wedding breakfast. This allows nervous speakers to get their speeches 'out of the way' so they can relax and enjoy the occasion. However, most toastmasters and other wedding advisors counsel against this as tight catering schedules can be severely disrupted if speeches go on for longer than intended. Guests also tend to be more receptive to speeches after having consumed a glass or two during the meal. And if there is no obvious highlight at the end of the meal, things can tend to fizzle out as individuals and groups of people migrate to the bar, smoking areas and elsewhere. For these reasons, it is better for the speeches to take place *after* people have eaten.

Knowing your purpose

The main purpose of a wedding speech is to propose a toast or to respond to one, or to do both, and the golden rule to remember is that *all speeches at wedding receptions are just elongated toasts.* The variable in the matter is how much you intend to say between your opening and closing words. This is the usual sequence.

- *Speech 1:* The father of the bride proposes a toast to the bride and groom.

- *Speech 2:* The bridegroom responds to the toast and later proposes a toast to the bridesmaids.

- *Speech 3:* The best man responds to the second toast on behalf of the bridesmaids (and any other attendants) and later may propose another toast to the bride and groom.

A brief history of toasts

The origin of the very first toast is uncertain, though it may well have developed out of mutual mistrust. In ancient Greece one of the preferred ways of dealing with social and domestic problems such as business disputes, family feuds or divorce was to invite people for a 'reconciliatory' goblet of wine, to tell them that life was too short for disputes, and then to seriously shorten their lives by administering hemlock to their drink. This gave a whole new meaning to the expression, 'What's your poison?'

Before too long people cottoned on to this pernicious practice and decided to think twice before imbibing, thereby maximising their chance of surviving long enough to order a chariot home. And yet it would have been incredibly impolite not to drink what you had been served. The solution to this moral dilemma was for the host to take the first drink after the wine was poured from a single bottle or decanter. If he didn't keel over, the guests could be assured the wine was safe for them to drink, too – as they tossed back a preliminary sip from their own goblets. This, then, was the beginning of the notion of 'drinking to your health'.

Burnt offerings

The actual term 'toast' appears to have derived from the Roman practice of dropping some burnt bread into a large bowl of wine as a way of removing undesirable flavours from the beverage. In particular, the cremated crust reduced the wine's acidity, making it more palatable – especially if it happened to be from one of those 'Buy 3 for 12,000 Lira' deals in the first place. After that, the bowl would be passed around and shared by all the guests. Towards the end of the evening, the host would be expected to say a few words in honour of his guests before drinking the dreaded dregs and ceremonially consuming that now saturated and soggy piece of toast.

We now fast-forward to 17th-century Britain, where toasting had become the norm in civilised society. At this time the position of toastmaster was introduced to ensure everyone had a fair chance to have their say, and the custom of drinking to absent friends was borrowed from Scandinavia. Interestingly, in the 1600s the word 'toast' was extended to refer to the wine glass containing the toast. Later, the meaning was stretched even further to refer to the act of drinking itself, and then further still to refer to the entire ritual and even to a person or persons being honoured.

At weddings today, toasts are as normal a part of a meal as eating with utensils and spilling peas on the floor. Participants and guests alike continue to go through all the motions of what appears to be a sort of secular communion. Not that there's anything wrong with that. Far from it. Perhaps we could do with a few more customs that bring us together in such spontaneous acts of community.

Toasting etiquette

The reason the father of the bride traditionally has the honour of opening proceedings and proposing the first toast is that he would have paid for wedding and, as host, it was considered appropriate that he spoke first. In reality, though, nowadays less than 20% of couples rely entirely on the bride's dad for funding – and almost two-thirds of them pay for everything themselves. Nevertheless, the tradition largely remains and it is still considered polite and courteous to invite him to speak first, followed, in turn, by the groom and his best man.

However, there are no rules that demand that those who traditionally make the speeches must actually do so. So don't let the thought of making a speech ruin your enjoyment of the wedding preparations and the day itself. If you wish, you could ask another family member or close friend of the family to speak on your behalf, especially if you are the father of the bride. Nobody should ever be forced to address the guests, if they do not want to. This is a happy day, so no one should be forced into doing anything.

It's a family affair

Given the complexity of many family units and the greater independence of people today, it is becoming more and more common for others to want to say a few words on the Big Day, too. There is no traditional order for these additional speakers because their contributions are a comparatively recent innovation and etiquette has yet to catch up and form a view.

That said, most wedding experts agree that if anyone else is going to speak, it is best that they do so *after* the groom but *before* the best man, who traditionally ends proceedings on a humorous high. If the bride is going to speak, she could do so jointly with her husband, or immediately before or after him. Although there is no toasting tradition here, it would seem reasonable that any other additional speakers should propose a toast to the bride and groom, and to anyone else they may have spoken of favourably – or at least they should wind up by wishing them all the best for the future.

Another point of etiquette to bear in mind is that if one or both of the happy couple are from different ethnic or cultural backgrounds, it is quite possible that different or additional people may be expected to speak – and possibly in a different order. If you are in any doubt, ask. It is important to get this right. Are there are any wedding conventions and rituals in respect to the speeches that you should be aware of? If there are, there will be scope for a fantastic and futuristic fusion of etiquette, custom and tradition.

The important thing is that the toastmaster, or the person fulfilling this pivotal role, must know in advance precisely who is going to be speaking, and in what order.

Staying on message

While every wedding speech should include a few sincere, optimistic and entertaining words, etiquette demands there are some subtle differences in the messages expected from each of the main speakers. We will consider this in more detail in Chapters 5 to 8. However, in broad terms, they can be summarised as follows.

Bride's father

Traditionally, he will thank everyone who has contributed to the wedding and to everyone who has come to the wedding, especially if they have travelled a long distance. The main theme of his speech will be his beloved daughter and his feelings as he now passes her over to the love and care of another man. He will also be expected to formally welcome his new son-in-law – together with his immediate family – into the clan, before adding some possibly amusing and personalised thoughts about love and marriage.

Bridegroom

This is really a general 'thank you' speech. It also provides you with a golden opportunity to make a public declaration of your love and to relate a touching or humorous story or two, perhaps about how you first met, how romance blossomed, your first meal together, or maybe the proposal.

Best man

He is expected to be the joker in the pack – but he should also include plenty of praise and congratulatory thoughts about the happy couple. If you turn serious towards the end, saying how much the groom really means to you as a valued friend – the audience will be spellbound.

Other speakers

Etiquette and tradition place less demand upon other speakers as there is little or no precedent to follow. However, it seems reasonable that if anyone is speaking *instead* of a 'main' speaker, he or she should convey a similar message and propose a similar toast as those that would have been expected of that speaker.

On the other hand, if someone is speaking *in addition* to the 'big three', there is no such historic burden of collective anticipation because contributions by the bride, her mother, her chief bridesmaid, step-parents, a child of the bride or groom or others are relatively new developments in terms of wedding procedure, and etiquette and expectation are yet to be established. Therefore they have far more freedom to say pretty much what they like, so long as it is upbeat and positive.

Being yourself

So those are the messages expected of the speakers. However, if you are a father of the bride who will cry uncontrollably if he keeps it too lovey-dovey, a groom who wants to say something a little more meaningful and memorable, or a best man who wants to make it more heartfelt – then do what feels right and comfortable. Don't lose sight of your speech's tradition by including some expected crowd-pleasers, but equally importantly be yourself and say what you truly feel.

Saying the right things

Choice of material is crucial. While every wedding speech should contain some sincere, optimistic and entertaining words, each of the main speakers should select just the right anecdotes, quotations and jokes to support their overall message and to give the audience what they want and expect.

It is a good idea for all the speakers to meet – or at least keep in contact, possibly by email, text or phone – to ensure that there is no duplication of jokes, stories or other material. It could be a little embarrassing if two or more speakers each describe how the happy couple met – especially if their versions differ.

However, that does not mean you should read each others' speeches; it simply means knowing you are not going to be talking about exactly the same thing as anyone else. Also, the best man should be a little sneaky here by withholding details of some of the stories he is going to relate about the groom. These should not be known by anyone in advance and should therefore be a surprise to everyone on the Big Day.

We've been here before

If it is a second or subsequent marriage, it is perfectly acceptable for a speaker to make a passing reference to the fact, but never to dwell on it. However, if either or both of the couple have children from a previous relationship, it is important not to hurt the youngsters' feelings.

The best advice in this situation is not to mention the ex-partner or relationship, but to make sure the children are not only mentioned, but also warmly welcomed into the new family. Children can easily recognise or perceive favouritism, so if there is more than one child involved, make sure each is welcomed equally enthusiastically. Roll out the red carpet for *all* of them.

Absent friends

It is common – though not universal – for the father of the bride to mention any people who were influential during his daughter's formative years – or possibly during the groom's – but who are unable to attend, perhaps because they live far away or because of illness. A potentially tricky situation arises when a close friend or family member is seriously ill or has recently died. Once again, it is perfectly acceptable to mention this, if you want to – and if you have agreed this in advance with those closest to the person concerned. Simply be tactful and respectful in what you say, before returning to the celebratory theme of your speech.

Alternatively, the groom could make this toast. This would be particularly appropriate if one or more of the couple's parents is ill or has recently died. However, under other circumstances, most wedding etiquette experts agree that the age and maturity of the father of the bride gives him the gravitas necessary to make this sometimes necessarily sober and thoughtful toast.

Getting everyone's names right

Make sure you get everyone's names right. A father may be used to linking his daughter's name with that of her sister or brother ('Debbie, Ray, be quiet!'). At the reception it is therefore all too easy for him to marry his daughter off to the wrong person ('I am delighted that Debbie and Ray have today tied the knot.'). Your family may find this faux pas amusing; the groom and his family may not be quite so sure. If you find you are making a similar error as you rehearse your speech, make sure you name the groom first.

Not embarrassing anyone

Your wedding speech is a time for celebration, and holding centre stage does not entitle you to hijack the proceedings. So don't embarrass the bride or groom by mentioning old flames, and never use the opportunity to have a go at a former partner. If you can't say anything nice, don't say anything at all.

Getting the tone right

This is an important day for all concerned. People want and expect plenty of encouraging thoughts and heartening messages. Your speech should help provide them. It should have the following qualities.

Optimistic and congratulatory

This is not a time to share your personal woes, paint a gloomy picture of the present or offer dire predictions about the future. Every wedding speaker should be upbeat and positive in what they say. Even the most humorous best man's roasting remarks should be sugared with sincere praise.

Heartfelt

Honesty is what they want. Convey your genuine feelings to the audience. The key word here is 'genuine'. False heartiness, cheap sincerity and – worst of all – crocodile tears will be all too obvious to an audience. Clearly, the amount of emotion displayed must depend on the personality of the speaker and the relationship he or she has with the bride, the groom, or both of them.

If you want to convey your innermost feelings, but find this difficult, you could do so by expressing the thoughts of others. In other words, you could weave in a couple of meaningful quotations. However, remember that quotations are intended to promote smiles and nods rather than strong emotional reactions or helpless mirth. For that reason they should used sparingly: spread thinly, like caviar, not piled on liberally, like marmalade.

Quoting people can also sound pompous. Just give a couple of appropriate lines and do so in a very casual way, making it clear that you had to look it up, or giving the impression you're not absolutely sure of your source:

> *I am reminded of the wise words of Jane Austen – reminded, I should say, by Linda, who looked them up last night . . .*

Wasn't it Karl Marx ... or maybe it was Groucho Marx ... who said ...?

Enlivened with humour

Any speech will benefit from an injection of a little humour. You do not need to be a stand-up comedian, indeed you should not be. However, you should always allow the humorous side of your personality to shine through.

Everyone loves a good gag. If you can find a relevant joke you are onto a winner. It will relax the audience and you. Matching your choice of material to the nature of the guests is easy when the entire group know each other – and they all know the bride and groom. At a wedding reception, this is often not the case, so you must choose your jokes and one-liners with care. If you include unnecessary details or drag a story out, those not in the know will soon lose interest.

Let's assume that only half the crowd knows that the bridegroom, Dave, has been known to take the occasional sickie. There is no need to bore the others with a long build-up. One simple gag will do the job:

Poor old Dave. Off sick again all last week ... this time with a broken thermos flask.

Now everyone should find that amusing – with the possible exception of Dave – and his (soon-to-be ex-) boss, if present.

Not outstaying your welcome

You won't make your speech immortal by making it everlasting. In the Bible, the story of the Creation is told in 400 words (that's about three minutes) and the Ten Commandments are covered in less than 300.

If you are one of the 'big three' (or speaking on behalf of one of them), try to say everything you need to in around five to ten minutes. If you are an 'additional' speaker, it would be courteous not to risk stealing anyone's thunder by speaking for longer than the main contributors. The exceptions to this 'rule' are a parent of the groom and the bride herself. Etiquette and common sense would certainly permit them to speak for about as about long as their counterparts, the father of the bride and the bridegroom.

Size does matter. And no speech can be entirely bad if it's short enough. Don't make the mistake of starting your speech at 1 o'clock *sharp* and ending it a 2 o'clock *flat*. Stand up to be seen; speak up to be heard; shut up to be appreciated.

2

Preparing a Great Speech

A great wedding speech is like a gourmet meal. Its opening lines should serve up a tasty little starter that really whets the audience's appetite for a mouth-watering main course. And its closing words should provide a delectable and memorable dessert with a delicious aftertaste.

There is no such thing as the best opening lines, the best middle section, or the best closing lines for a speech, because every speech – and every speaker – is different. In this chapter you will learn a number of techniques that can be used to open and close a speech and keep the middle section entertaining and relevant.

We will then consider how to keep it all flowing gracefully from beginning to end and how best to prepare your all-important script. All these methods and approaches are tried and tested, so you don't need to worry about choosing a dud. Study the options and decide what would work best for *your* speech – and for *you*.

Grabbing their attention

There are dozens of ways to put over a great opening line. It's just a matter of finding the pattern of words that suits your style and has exactly the effect you are after. Work on your opening until you've got it spot on. Then memorise it. You must know precisely how you are going to open your speech. There is absolutely no room for any ad-libbing here.

It is vital to have an opening line that really grabs your audience's attention. Entertainers call this having a hook. The four best of these are:

- hooking with humour;
- hooking with a quotation;
- hooking with anniversaries;
- hooking with brackets.

Your opening words help set the tone of your entire speech. So don't start with a joke unless you intend to continue largely in that same humorous vein. Similarly, don't open with an emotional quotation unless the rest of your speech is essentially to be warm, tender and sentimental in nature.

The bride's father can begin directly with one of these hooks, but the bridegroom and best man should remember to thank the previous speaker immediately before or soon after hooking their audience. Additional speakers may wish to thank the bride and groom for asking or allowing them to speak. However, to avoid boring repetition, in the examples that follow, I have included such thanks with the first hook only.

Hooking with humour

Opening with a short and relevant joke, anecdote or one-liner will help to relax you and get the audience laughing and even more on your side than they are already. However, it would be somewhat bizarre to open with a joke if the remainder of your speech is almost entirely serious. Such a hook is therefore often – though not exclusively – best suited to a jokey best man.

Here are some possibilities:

Ladies and Gentlemen, the last time I made a wedding speech someone at the rear shouted, 'I can't hear you!' – and a man sitting next to me yelled back, 'I'll change places with you!' Thank you, [groom], *for those lovely words about the beautiful bridesmaids...*

Ladies and Gentlemen, the last time I made a wedding speech a man fell asleep. I asked a pageboy to wake him, and do you know what the little horror replied? He said, 'You wake him. You were the one who put him to sleep.'

Ladies and Gentlemen, before I start speaking I have something to say.

[After a formal introduction by a toastmaster] *Ladies and Gentlemen, did he say pray* **for** *the silence of* [your name]?

[After being called upon to give an impromptu speech] *Ladies and Gentlemen, I am totally unprepared for this, but, as Big Ben said to the Leaning Tower of Pisa, 'I've got the time if you've got the inclination.'*

Hooking with a quotation

Here you simply begin your wedding speech with a short and relevant quotation. It is far safer to use a serious quote rather than a cynical one. There are thousands, perhaps millions of possibilities available to you. Here are just a few of them to give you an idea of how they can best be used to open a speech:

Ladies and Gentlemen, 'Love is a great force in life; it is indeed the greatest of all things.' So said E.M. Forster, and E.M. knew what he was talking about . . .

Ladies and Gentlemen, it has been said that, 'success in marriage is more than **finding** *the right person; it is* **being** *the right person'. Well, I can tell you with one hundred per cent confidence and conviction that* [bride] *has not only* **found** *the right person . . . she* **is** *the right person . . .'*

Ladies and Gentlemen, as the poet Keats reminds us, 'Love is the light and sunshine of life and we cannot fully enjoy ourselves or anything else, unless someone we love enjoys it with us.' Well, from today [bride] *and* [groom] *are certain to enjoy a wonderful life together . . .*

15

Ladies and Gentlemen, a wise man once remarked that, 'marriage is like wine; it gets better with age'. Well, with that intoxicating thought in mind, I'm sure we are all absolutely delighted that [bride] *and* [groom] *have finally tied the knot here today ...*

Sometimes a quotation associated with the bride's or bridegroom's occupation can be adapted to make an excellent and original opening. For example, here are a couple of adaptations suitable for members of the armed services. A speaker with a reasonable voice could even sing the first of them.

Ladies and Gentlemen, 'When he was a lad he served a term. As an office boy to an Attorney's firm. He cleaned the windows and he swept the floor. And he polished up the handle of the big front door. He polished up that handle so carefullee. That now he's the Ruler of the Queen's Navee' – well, almost, anyway.

Ladies and Gentlemen, 'Some talk of Alexander, and some of Hercules, of Hector and Lysander and such great names as these.' But I would rather talk about [bride and groom].

Hooking with anniversaries

Another wonderful way of grabbing an audience is to tell them that 'Today's the day!', not only because of the recent marriage but also because of other things that happened in years gone by. It is best to mention two things as well as the marriage – probably a famous person's birth and a second memorable event.

As always, use your own words, but this is the sort of thing you should say:

Ladies and Gentlemen, this is a day heavy with significance! This very day, the 21st of July, will always be associated with three truly memorable events. Funnyman Robin Williams was born in 1952; Neil Armstrong took a giant leap for mankind in 1969; and on this day in 201X, [groom] *married* [bride]*! So in 1969 it was Neil Armstrong, but today it is* [groom] *who is over the moon.*

Hooking with brackets

Bracketing is a device usually associated with seasoned pros. It requires far more thought and planning than the other hooks because it is designed not only to grab an audience's attention at the *start* of a speech, but also – and at the same time – to set up a situation that can be exploited at the *end*. The idea is to present your speech as a satisfying whole, not just as a series of jokes, quotes and sentimental reminiscences.

The two brackets consist of a *set-up* at the opening of the speech and a *pay-off* at the end. The words you will end with include those planted clearly at the start, like this:

Set-up: *Ladies and Gentlemen, as Rafael left the church today I heard him ask the vicar if he'd be committing a sin if he played tennis on the Sabbath. The vicar replied, 'The way you play, it would be a sin on any day.' But Rafael is improving. He practises by hitting a tennis ball against his garage door. It's really improved his game. He hasn't won yet, but last week he took the door to five sets.*

Pay-off: *Rafael and Serena are excellent tennis players who are both game and set for the perfect match.*

Notice the repetition of the planted words 'Rafael' and 'tennis'. This helps the open-and-closed nature of the brackets and provides a pleasing symmetry.

You can get ideas for humorous, romantic or sentimental brackets simply by listening to songs composed by the best popular lyricists of yesterday and today: Noel Coward, Ira Gershwin, Cole Porter, Jim Webb, Bob Dylan, Ray Davies, Lou Reed, Morrisey – to name but a few. This is how master songsmith Sammy Cahn achieved a neat little twist in the tail of *Call Me Irresponsible*:

Set-up: *Call me irresponsible, call me unreliable, throw in undependable too.*

Pay-off: *Call me irresponsible, yes I'm unreliable, but it's undeniably true: I'm irresponsibly mad for you.*

If you make use of a lyricist's brackets, always reword them into the kind of language you use, making sure that they no longer rhyme. In this way your audience won't recognise your source – or your sauce – and you are sure to come across as a natural and original speaker.

It is quite easy to adapt and paraphrase musical brackets to suit your speech. Let's take a more up-to-date example. These are the set-up and pay-off lines used by Rupert Holmes in *Nearsighted*:

Set-up: *If you take these glasses from my face I think that you will find I'm undeniably, certifiably just a shade of blind. The day is brighter, somewhat lighter, when it's slightly blurred. Nearsighted, it's another lovely day, so I stumble on my way.*

Pay-off: *Nearsighted: loving life is such a breeze. Nearsighted: I see just what I please – and it pleases me to see you. Though I'm slightly out of focus, I can see my dreams come true. Nearsighted, all I need to see is you.*

This is how a bespectacled groom might adapt, develop and paraphrase these brackets:

Set-up: *Ladies and Gentlemen, if I take off my glasses I can't see very far ahead. In the past I've often been shortsighted and stumbled my way through life. But today I can see the way ahead clearly.*

Pay-off: *You know, I don't need these glasses to see a bright future for us. Shortsighted?* [remove your glasses] *Who cares? All I need to see is you.*

Bracketing is a wonderful way of linking attention-grabbing openings with emotion-packed big finishes.

Getting the middle section right

The starter is now well prepared and it is time to turn attention to the main course. Recipe for a great little speech? Not too cheesey, no waffle and plenty of shortening. The ingredients required are just the right balance of seriousness and humour and, if you are the bride's dad or her new hubbie, don't forget to apply them all with liberal helpings of sentiment.

This central part of your speech is where you need to convey your overall positive upbeat message. As we have seen, at a wedding reception there are some subtle differences in the messages that are expected of different speakers and there will be more specific and targeted advice about this throughout the relevant chapters.

Once you have decided upon which jokes you are going to tell and which short stories you are going to relate, work on each of them in isolation. You'll find out how to link them all together to form a graceful, unbroken, flowing speech towards the end of this chapter. And please remember: the earlier you start on this, the more good ideas are likely to come to you.

While every speech, and every speaker is different, there are some features and characteristics that are common to the middle sections of all successful wedding speeches, regardless of who is speaking. Successful speakers always recognize the importance of:

- providing valleys and peaks;
- keeping everything relevant;
- involving the audience.

Let's consider each, in turn.

Providing valleys and peaks

Your audience would soon suffer from sensory overload if your every utterance demanded roars of laughter or floods of tears. Less really is more.

Of course people want a good laugh and they love to be emotionally hit for six by something unexpected or thought-provoking you may say. However, they also want times when they can just sit back, relax and quietly reflect upon your words of wit and wisdom.

Just as the varied rhythm and intensity of a fireworks display adds anticipation and excitement, so a landscape of valleys and peaks keeps an audience interested and involved. Your speech needs a varied texture. It needs to have light and shade, highs and lows. People need valleys before they can see peaks.

So by all means use some of the techniques described below to keep your audience involved and to provide those all-important highs, but also remember to talk to your audience in the same straightforward way as you would talk to John and Jane Smith. What is your audience, after all, other than a collection of John and Jane Smiths? And the best way to do this is to include plenty of everyday, chatty, conversational English – because that is the language of easy communication. And easy communication is what effective speechmaking is all about.

Keeping everything relevant

To keep people interested and involved, everything you say should be strictly relevant, meaningful and unique to *this* couple, to *this* wedding and to *this* audience. In the same way that no woman wants to go to a wedding wearing the same dress as anyone else, no speaker should want to go to a reception making the same speech as anyone else.

Real-life stories are unbeatable. You dream it as you tell it, drawing others along with you, and in this way memory and imagination and language combine to create spirits in the mind. The stories you choose should all have a telling point; illustrating, for example, how dependable the bride is, how undependable the groom is, how much they love each other. If you know just the right story which portrays precisely what you want to portray, work on it and then tell it with purpose, pride and passion. If you don't, ask friends, family and work colleagues for their memories. Choose the right story and the room will get goosebumps.

Adapting and personalising material

When it comes to humour, speakers have far more freedom and latitude. While the anecdotes you relate should be true (perhaps being slightly embellished for effect), jokes can be made up, so long as they sound as though they *could* be true.

Once you are satisfied that a joke would work well in your speech, perhaps because it reflects nicely one of the groom's characteristics or foibles, or the best man's looks or personality, or maybe the bride's job or hobby, you will need to adapt it, that is, make a few changes here and there until it is meaningful to your audience. For example, if you want to tell a joke about a taxi driver you might well be able to adapt one about a bus driver or a lorry driver. Any gag involving motor vehicles or a long road journey could probably apply to any of them.

Then you must personalise your material. Don't tell a story about a taxi driver – any old taxi driver – tell one about a particular taxi driver, probably about the bride, the bridegroom, the best man or you. Don't talk about 'a town', mention *your* town. And don't say, 'he drove down a back street', say, 'Lloyd drove down Inkerman Street.' In other words, give your audience enough local details so they can actually see the events unfold as you describe them – even if only in their mind's eye.

Involving the audience

Your aim is to communicate with your audience – to establish a dialogue with them – to turn listeners into participants. How? By involving them. By allowing them not only to hear your speech but also to *experience* it.

For Aaron Sorkin, writer of the hit television drama *The West Wing*, 'Great language has exactly the same properties as great music. It has rhythm, it has pitch, it has tone, it has accents.' Listen to great raconteurs and speechmakers to see how they do it. Sir Peter Ustinov brought his anecdotes and reminiscences to life, giving them a lyrical, almost magical quality. You can do the same by:

- painting word pictures;
- using colourful language;
- engaging all the senses;
- using symbolism;
- remembering rhythm.

Don't worry: no speaker will ever use all these techniques in the same speech. Just study and practise the options available to see which ones work best for you. Then make the rest of your speech far more straightforward, conversational and chatty. In this way you provide your guests with the best of both worlds: a speech which is not only easy to follow, but one also certain to involve, to engage – and at times to truly move them.

Painting word pictures

Watching a story unfold before your eyes is dramatic and memorable. The characters move. The scenes are in colour. The whole thing has life. Specific detail allows an audience to see the scenes you are describing. This means avoiding vague references to *food* and replacing them with *pizzas* or *kebabs*. To say a meal was *delicious* merely tells them you enjoyed it. Use adjectives that conjure up specific images and trigger the senses: a *spicy* curry, a *fruity* jelly, a *savoury* pie.

The best writers of popular fiction know they must paint word pictures. This comes from *Fallen Curtain* by Ruth Rendell:

I loved visiting gran's. Tea was lovely, fish and chips that gran didn't fetch from the shop but cooked herself, cream meringues and chocolate eclairs, tinned peaches with evaporated milk, the lot washed down with fizzy lemonade.

Can't you just feel that gassy pop getting up your nose?

Use imagery when you crack a joke too. Don't tell the gag, paint it:

Soon after we met, [groom] *invited me to his eighteenth birthday party and he gave me details of his address and how to get there. He said, 'A number 8 bus will bring you right to my door – 117 Alma Road. Walk up to the front door and press the doorbell with your elbow.' 'Why my elbow?' I asked. 'Because you'll have the wine in one hand and my prezzie in the other, won't you?'*

One mental picture is worth a thousand words.

Using colourful language

No, not that kind of language! Try to make your speech colourful and original. Similes and metaphors are particularly useful. A **simile** is a figure of speech, usually introduced by 'like' or 'as', that compares one thing to another:

She was simmering *like* a corked volcano.

I am as awkward *as* a cow on ice.

Because a simile's function is comparison, it is not as evocative as a metaphor. A **metaphor** is more subtle and revealing, not simply comparing but transforming one thing into another. The right metaphor can really lift a wedding speech. Take a look at this example:

Marriage. Ever since humans gathered together in caves they – we – have displayed a basic instinct for becoming couples. Your man and your woman. Your Romeo and your Juliet. Your yin and your yang. It's as natural as his and her bath towels. If the life of humankind were music they would all be duets. It's been a bit of a musical day one way and another.

Violins in harmony with cellos. [Bride] *in harmony with* [groom]. *The past in harmony with the future. And, as the Bard of Avon put it: 'If music be the food of love, rock on.'*

And how about this?

With the two of us it is just as it is with the honeysuckle that attaches itself to the hazel tree: when it has wound and attached itself around the trunk, the two can survive together; but if someone tries to separate them, the hazel dies quickly and the honeysuckle with it. Sweet love, so it is with us: you cannot live without me, nor I without you.

That was said by Marie de France over 800 years ago – and it works just as well today. The past in harmony with the present.

Another useful figure of speech is **hyperbole**, or deliberately overstating your argument:

I've told you millions of times not to exaggerate.

In a wedding speech you can get away with saying things that most people would find embarrassing and even crass in everyday conversation:

You are the best parents/son/daughter in the world.

Not only can you get away with it – such bizarre overstatement can be highly effective, bringing a lump to the throat and a tear to the eye:

I'll love you till the ocean is folded and hung up to dry, and the seven stars go squawking like geese about the sky.

Engaging all the senses

Sensory details bring breadth and depth to your descriptions. Again, we can learn a lot from the best writers of popular fiction. This is how Stephen King brought a character to life in *Carrie*:

*Norma led them around the dance floor to their table. She exuded odours
of Avon soap, Woolworth's perfume and Juicy Fruit gum.*

I bet you can see Norma. Your vision of her may be different from mine but
she's there all the same, and that's all that matters.

And how about this from Katherine Mansfield:

Alexander and his friend in a train. Spring ... wet lilac ... spouting rain.

So few words yet the wetness is palpable.

In her autobiography, *Walled Gardens*, Annabel Davis-Doff shows how a
scent can bring back memories of childhood:

*Recently, my mother and I were visiting my brother at his house near
Dublin and walking through his tiny greenhouse. I reached out to a tomato
plant and nipped a shoot between my thumbnail and first finger, the way
my father did to prune out the small redundant leafy growths which sprout
between the main trunk and branches of the plant. Without showing it to
her, I held the strong-smelling leaves close to my mother's face.*

'What does that remind you of?' I asked.

*'Grenville,' she said, without a moment's pause or any sign of surprise at
my question.*

*It made me feel close to my mother, as though I hadn't left home so long
ago or gone so far away. On a warm July afternoon in Dublin she thinks
the same thing, when she catches the scent of tomato plants, that I do in
my garden in Connecticut.*

As you speak, try to involve your audience. Allow them to do far more than
just listen to you. Help them to *hear*, to *see*, to *smell*, to *touch*, to *taste*. Allow
them to *experience* your speech.

Using symbolism

Symbolism is the technique of apparently describing something small and insignificant, when really referring to something far more fundamental and important. Advertising agencies spend thousands researching this device. Let us see what we can learn from them.

How often have you seen actors wearing white coats and glasses discussing the merits of a product in a laboratory setting? These are symbols which represent the medical and scientific research professions and are meant to imply that the product has been approved by, and has the support of doctors, scientists and researchers.

Bah, humbug? Maybe, but it works. You'll find symbols in all adverts. The colour red crops up a lot, like a red sunset to advertise a liqueur, or a bunch of red roses behind a bottle of perfume. Red is warm. It is vibrant, a symbol of passion, excitement and romance. When you want to suggest these things, describe a variety of hot colours, especially red.

The seasons of the year and the weather are potent symbols too. The image of a damp autumn evening is depressing while a warm spring afternoon is associated with new life, new beginnings. Writer Henry James said the two most beautiful words in the English language are 'summer afternoon' because they evoke just the right emotions. Did you notice the reference to 'a warm July afternoon' in Annabel Davis-Doff's reminiscence? Make use of such powerful symbols in your speech. Go for it. Tug at the heartstrings. Touch the heart:

> I took a walk in the park this morning. Every bush, every tree trembled with the fluttering of butterflies – beautiful red butterflies. It was magnificent. Yesterday there were no butterflies in my garden. Today there are thousands. Tomorrow there will be millions.

Using words colourfully and creatively will bring the middle of your speech to life like a shot of whisky in a cup of coffee.

Remembering rhythm

A good speech should attract and hold listeners as a magnet attracts and holds iron filings. Here are four simple techniques that can turn your words into music to an audience's ears.

1. The rule of three

   Three is a magic number. People love to hear speakers talk to the beat of three. The effect of three words, three phrases or three sentences is powerful and memorable:

   Marriage is the meeting of two minds . . . of two hearts . . . of two souls.

   May you be blessed with happiness that grows . . . with love that deepens . . . and with peace that endures.

   We wish you fun and excitement for today . . . hopes and dreams for tomorrow . . . and love and happiness forever.

2. Parallel sentences

   Sentences that are parallel add a rhythmic beauty that helps an audience anticipate and follow your thoughts:

   Marriage is a celebration of love. Marriage is a celebration of life. Marriage is a celebration of joy. As you walk through life, hold hands and never let go.

3. Alliteration

   The recurrence of sounds and syllables, usually at the beginning of words, can help create just the right mood:

   Water your garden with friendship, faith and favour. And then watch it grow. You deserve a garden of love.

4. Repetition

   If there is anything that is almost guaranteed to make an audience break out into spontaneous applause it is a repetition of strong, emotive words:

I will love you for ever . . . and ever . . . and ever!

However, use the wrong words and it will fall flat. How does this sound?

I will think the world of you indefinitely . . . indefinitely . . . indefinitely!

It doesn't work, does it?

Ending on a high

With the first two courses now well prepared, it is time to move on to the dessert, the culmination of your culinary creations. Film producer Sam Goldwyn once told a scriptwriter: 'What we want is a story that starts with an earthquake and works its way up to a climax.' It's the same with your speech. You have opened with a great hook and seamlessly moved into the main body of your speech, giving them some stories and reminiscences which strike just the right balance of seriousness and humour. Now it is time to deliver a final round verbal knock-out.

The ending, like the opening, is far too important to leave to the mercy of chance or the whim of the moment. You need to plan it carefully and then memorise it. Try to end with a flourish. Your concluding remarks should be to a speaker what a high note is to a singer: the candescence that triggers spontaneous cheers and applause. If you can find your ideal ending, you will inject that ultimate bit of magic.

As well as the bracketing hook close which, by definition, should already include a big finish, the humour hook, quotation hook and anniversary hook can all easily be adapted to serve as powerful or amusing closes. Here is an example of each. On the day, you will also need to include a concluding toast. However, to avoid repetition, I have made reference to this in the first example only.

Ladies and Gentlemen, in conclusion I must admit that I have made a very similar speech to this before. Once to the patients in Broadmoor, once to

Aberdeen Naturalists' Group, and once to Penzance Haemorrhoid Sufferers Society – a stand-up buffet. So to those of you who have now heard these words four times, I sincerely apologise. And now, may I propose a toast to . . .

It has been said that: 'there is only one happiness in life: to love and be loved'. Today [bride] and [groom] found their happiness.

This day, the 18th of December, will always be remembered because of three famous events. Slavery was abolished in America in 1865, film director Steven Spielberg was born back in 1947, and on this very day in 201X, [groom] married [bride].

There are four other classic closes, any of which would help make your wedding speech memorable. These are:

- the sentimental close;
- the inspirational close;
- the shock close;
- the wit and wisdom close.

Let's take a look at each in turn.

The sentimental close

This is a close that can work wonderfully for the bridegroom or the bride's father. If you mean it deeply, then say it from the heart:

[Bride], *I love you.*

The inspirational close

We can learn much from the great inspirational speakers of past and present: Sir Winston Churchill, John F. Kennedy, Nelson Mandela, Barack Obama. If you can find an ideal uplifting line that would wrap up your speech perfectly, then grab it, adapt it and use it.

Martin Luther King concluded his famous 'I have a dream' speech with these immortal words:

Free at last! Free at last! Thank God Almighty, Free at last!

This powerful three-phrase close could be adapted to:

Together at last! Together at last! Thank God, we're together at last!

The shock close

The idea here is to make an apparently outrageous or shocking statement. Then, after a brief pause, to clarify yourself. Your audience's relief will be audible.

*Finally, I have a confession to make. When I took my vows in church today, I lied. I did **not** marry for better or for worse . . . I married for good.*

The wit and wisdom close

Some speakers end with a good joke while others prefer to impart a pearl of wisdom. Why not do both? Why not use humour to illustrate a universal truth? These three gems come from Bob Monkhouse, Groucho Marx and Pam Ayres:

Marriage is an investment that pays dividends if you pay interest.

Woman lies to man. Man lies to woman. But the best part is when they lie together.

Love is like a curry and I'll explain to you, that love comes in three temperatures: medium, hot and spicy vindaloo.

Whichever close you choose, make sure you end on a note of high emotion or with a witty, wise or uplifting little quote or story that will leave them gobsmacked. And finally, where appropriate, don't forget to propose that toast.

Proposing your toast

Once you have delivered your big finish, you could simply say something like:

Ladies and Gentlemen, I give you: the bride and groom.

Alternatively, you could add a short toast before inviting the guests to raise their glasses:

Ladies and Gentlemen, please join me in a toast to love and laughter, and happy ever after. Let's all drink to two wonderful people . . .

Shakespeare reminds us that brevity is the soul of wit. He forgot to add that it is also the soul of great toasts. Here are a few possibilities for general toasts to the bride and groom. Some suggestions for toasts particularly suited to each of the main speakers are offered in Chapters 5 to 7.

Here's to the groom with a bride so fair, Here's to the bride with a groom so rare.

May their joys be as bright as the morning, and their sorrows but shadows that fade in the sunlight of love.

Here's a toast to a couple who share a love of life. May they, from this day forth, share a life of love.

Keeping it flowing

Once you have planned a great opening, a humorous or emotionally charged big finish and toast, and a series of beautiful, funny and moving stories and reminiscences to fill the middle section of your speech, you will need to link them all together to form a satisfying whole. There are a number of techniques that can help you to do this.

Have you noticed how entertainers, politicians and TV presenters move easily and unobtrusively from one topic to another? Like them, you can make your speech flow smoothly and gracefully from beginning to end by making use of a few simple devices, such as:

- bridges;
- triggers;
- rhetorical questions;
- flashbacks;
- identifiers;
- lists;
- pauses;
- physical movement;
- quotations, anecdotes and jokes.

Let us briefly consider each in turn.

A *bridge* is a word that alerts an audience that you are changing direction or moving to a new thought:

> *She took the job in London.* Meanwhile *other developments were taking place . . .*

A *trigger* is a repetition of the same word or phrase to link one topic with another.

> *That was what* [groom] **was like** *at school. Now I'll tell you what he* **was like** *at college . . .*

A *rhetorical question* – a question which does not require an answer – is another useful device to help keep a speech flowing.

That's what makes our marriage so happy. So what advice can I offer to the newlyweds?...

Some members of the audience will know both the bride and the groom very well while others may only know one of them. Asking a rhetorical question is also an excellent way of telling people something while not insulting the intelligence of those already in the know.

What can I tell you about a man who won the school prize for economics, represented the county at hockey and passed his driving test... at the sixth attempt?

A *flashback* is a sudden shift to the past to break what seems to be a predictable narrative:

She was born in...

She went to school at...

She got her first job with... (yawn, yawn!)

It would have been far more interesting to have provided an unexpected flashback link, such as:

Today she is the attractive, sophisticated lady you see before you. But ten years ago *she wasn't like that...*

An *identifier* is a word or phrase that keeps cropping up throughout a speech to help tie everything together. It also reinforces the audience's group identity.

Look at our [not *the*] *beautiful bride...*

We [not *I*] *wish them well...*

A *list* is a very simple way of combining apparently unrelated stories.

I remember three occasions when [groom] *got into trouble at school...*

But don't rely too heavily on lists because a catalogue of events soon becomes extremely tedious to listen to.

Pausing will show an audience that you have finished a section of your speech and are about to move on to another. This is a non-verbal link that can work very well so long as it's not overdone.

By *physically moving*, your body language can tell the audience that you are moving on to something new. If you turn to the bride, they will know you are going to talk to her, or about her.

Finally, a *quotation, anecdote* or *joke* can serve as an excellent link. Here a man-on-the-bus gag links a personal compliment about good manners with a more general observation that everyone has played their part in making this a day to remember:

> [Bride] *always shows good old-fashioned courtesy to her fellow human beings. A rare attribute today, I'm sure you'll agree. When she was on the bus last week she stood up to give an elderly gentleman her seat. He was so surprised he fainted. When he came round he said, 'Thank you,' and* [bride] *fainted. Well I'm delighted to say there has been absolutely no shortage of courtesy here today. Things could not have gone better . . .*

Preparing your script

The best speakers are natural, easy, fluent, friendly and amusing. No script for them. How could there be? They are talking only to us and basing what they say on our reactions as they go along. For most of us, however, that sort of performance is an aspiration rather than a description. Our tongues are not so honeyed and our words are less winged. We need a script.

But what kind of a script? That's for you to decide. There's no fixed way to do it. However, most successful speakers would agree that you will have to write and rewrite your speech several times before you're totally happy with it. Many of them would also advise you to begin with an **outline** – the broad areas and topics you want to cover. Then prepare your **first draft**. Leave it for a day or two before re-drafting it. Do this as often as is necessary until you are totally happy with your **final draft**. It's fine to jot down and later revise your speech on a few sheets of paper. However, it's far easier to add bits, delete bits and swap bits around, if you have access to a computer.

You can then either memorise your speech, decide to read it out at the reception, or summarise it using bullet points on cue cards. The first method may simply prove unrealistic for many speakers and the second approach could result in you spending your entire speech with your head buried in the paper rather than looking at the guests. For these reasons, many speakers favour **cue cards** incorporating a few memory-jogging keywords and phrases to ensure they can not only maintain a reasonable amount of eye contact with their audience, but also that they cover all the ground they intended to.

When you speak, it is important to get the wording of your opening and closing lines spot on. For that reason you should *memorise* them. However, it is far better to simply *familiarise* yourself with the middle section of your speech. In this way you are sure to come across as a far more natural and spontaneous speaker because you will be using your own words and phrases, not reciting a prepared speech. That's another reason why cue cards are so useful.

Thinking like a listener... and writing like a talker

If communication were to be expressed as a metaphor, it would be a busy motorway. Messages pass each way, some in the fast lane, others in the slow lane. But they always flow in two directions. Speaking and listening.

Most people can write something to be *read*; few can write something to be *said*. Indeed, most people are unaware that there is even a difference. We are used to writing things to be read: by our friends, our relatives, our bosses, our work colleagues. Such everyday written communication is known as **text**. What we are not used to doing is speaking our written words out loud.

Writing intended to be spoken and heard is known as **script**.

Every effective speechmaker *must* recognise that there are very important differences between text and script.

Text	**Script**
• is a journey at the reader's pace;	• is a journey at the speaker's pace;
• can be re-read, if necessary;	• is heard once, and once only;
• can be read in any order.	• is heard in the order it is spoken.

Therefore, you need to use words intended to be said, not read. You must prepare and present a speech for an audience which *cannot* listen at its own pace; which *cannot* ask you to repeat parts it did not hear or understand; and which *cannot* choose the order in which to consider your words.

We seem subconsciously to understand the best words and phrases and the best order of words and phrases when we speak, but we seem to lose the knack when we write script. Consider how the same sentiment might be conveyed by a writer, first using text and then script:

Text

The meaning of marriage is not to be found in church services, or in romantic novels or films. We have no right to expect a happy ending. The meaning of marriage is to be found in all the effort that is required to make a marriage succeed. You need to get to know your partner, and thereby to get to know yourself.

Script

The meaning of marriage isn't to be found in wedding bells ... it isn't the stuff of Mills and Boon romances . . . there is no happy ever after. No, the meaning of marriage is in the trying and it's about learning about someone else . . . and through that, learning about yourself.

The lesson is clear: Speak your words out loud before you commit them to paper. In this way, your script will be far more informal in tone and you will be talking to your audience, not writing to them. As you talk, you will find that each element, each phrase, each sentence, will be built from what has gone before. Instinctively, you will take your listeners from the *known* to the *unknown*; from the *general* to the *particular*; from the *present* to the *future*.

3 Getting Mentally Prepared

The speech has been planned and the script written. Half of the work is now behind you. What you must do now is relax and get yourself into the right frame of mind to deliver it. This means thinking positively, visualising success and learning how to deal with any sudden attack of nerves, both before and during your speech.

Of course, one of the most effective ways to stave off a virulent attack of the 'I'm-not-worthies' is to know you are well prepared. This means practising your speech until you're totally comfortable with every aspect of it. We'll therefore consider the importance of rehearsing in the next chapter.

Making fear your friend

Fear is nothing to be frightened of. People get nervous because they are afraid of failing, looking foolish and not living up to expectations. Nervousness is caused by the fear of looking ridiculous to others.

Few people claim to be able to speak without any nerves. Most will say that lack of nerves is not only unlikely, it is undesirable. They need the adrenaline to carry them along.

However, if you feel too nervous the quality of your speech will suffer. Remind yourself that your audience will be on your side. This is a happy day. They are not a jury. They are willing you to do well. And, quite frankly, they won't give a damn if you do fluff a line or two.

Whatever you do, don't drink too much. Booze is like success; it is great until it goes to your head. Slurred eulogies better suited to closing time at the Rovers, Vic or Woolpack are not what's required here. Bob Monkhouse's maxim was: never accept a drink *before* you speak; never refuse one *after*.

Thinking positively

Tell yourself that you are going to make a great speech. And *believe* it. The largely untapped power of positive thinking really is immense. Unfortunately, many speakers think they are going to fail, and this becomes a self-fulfilling prophecy. As Henry Ford put it: 'Whether you think you will succeed or whether you think you will fail, you will probably be right.'

Some people may find this anonymous poem inspirational. Needless to say, it applies equally to women.

IF

If you think you are beaten, you are;
If you think you dare not, you don't;
If you'd like to win, but think you can't,
It's almost certain you won't;
If you think you'll lose you've lost.
For out of the world we find
Success begins with a fellow's will –
It's all in the state of mind.
If you think you're outclassed, you are.
You've got to think high to rise;
You've got to be sure of yourself before
You can ever win a prize.
Life's battles don't always go
To the stronger or faster man,
But sooner or later the man who wins
Is the one who *thinks* he can.

Visualising success

Visualisation is the planting of mental images into the subconscious mind. These images must be vivid and real – you must be able to *see*, to *hear*, to *smell*, to *touch*, to *taste* and to truly *live them*. It is a way to free yourself from previously accepted boundaries and barriers. We are all victims of programming. As a child, you may have been told, 'your spelling is atrocious.' Your subconscious mind would have accepted this (even if it were not true) and it would have made sure that from that moment you really *were* a poor speller. Through visualisation you can reprogramme your subconscious mind to accept that you can spell well. In exactly the same way, you can pre-programme your subconscious mind to accept that you are not nervous and that you are going to make an excellent speech.

If you can vividly *imagine* an event happening, it will greatly strengthen the likelihood of it *actually* happening. This is not a crankish idea. Controlled medical experiments have proved it to be true. When a patient visualises cancer cells being engulfed by antibodies in the bloodstream, it is far more likely to happen than if that patient just lies back and lets nature take its course.

You are now going to watch a 'film clip' with a difference – because the screenwriter, the director and the star will be *you*. Close your eyes and visualise yourself rising to speak. You are looking good. Feel the warmth of the audience. You are surrounded by family and friends. You pause for a moment and then begin. They love your opening hook. But it gets better; your stories and little jokes wow them. Laughter one minute, tears the next. They are eating out of your hand. Then comes that emotion-packed big finish. Nobody could have topped that. Listen to their cheers and applause. Now that's what I call a wedding speech!

The best times to present your subconscious mind with such a positive visualisation is when you are mentally calm and physically relaxed, when you are in the hypnogogic state that precedes sleep, or when you are in a state of light sleep.

Using emergency relaxation techniques

However, if you still feel the pressure beginning to get to you, try some of these emergency relaxation techniques. See which ones work best for you. They can be used anywhere and at any time without anyone, except you, knowing it.

Breathing to reduce tension

1. Sit comfortably with your arms at your sides and breathe in deeply through your nose.

2. Hunch up your shoulders as high as you can, clench your fists, push your toes hard into the floor, tense your body even harder than it is now – and then still harder.

3. Hold your breath for a few seconds.

4. As you exhale slowly through your nose, loosen your shoulders and let them drop, unclench your fists and let your heels return to the floor. Imagine that your shoulders are dropping down as far as your waist and that your feet are so light that they are floating off the ground.

Sitting at a table

1. Pull in your stomach muscles tightly. Relax.

2. Clench your fists tightly. Relax.

3. Extend your fingers. Relax.

4. Grasp the seat of your chair. Relax.

5. Press your elbows tightly into the side of your body. Relax.

6. Push your feet into the floor. Relax.

Spot relaxation

1. Imagine that your shoulders are very heavy.

2. Hunch them up.

3. Drop them down very slowly.

4. Gently tip your head forward and feel the muscles pulling up through the middle of your shoulder blades.

5. Move your head gently backwards and feel the tension in the muscles down the front of your neck.

6. Bring your head back to an upright position and breathe very deeply for a few moments.

Stopping negative thoughts

1. Tell yourself '*Stop!*'

2. Breathe in and hold your breath.

3. Exhale slowly, relaxing your shoulders and hands.

4. Pause. Breathe in slowly, relaxing your forehead and jaw.

5. Remain quiet and still for a few moments.

Head in the clouds

1. Stare at the ceiling and visualise floating clouds.

2. Imagine you are drifting towards them.

3. Release your tension and watch it float away with the clouds.

4. Gradually return from the clouds, feeling calm, cool and collected in your thoughts.

Draining tension away

Imagine you are transparent and filled with your favourite colour liquid. The temperature is perfect. Then drain the liquid from your body through your fingers and toes. Feel the tension draining away with the fluid.

The decanter

Sit comfortably and imagine that your body is a decanter. The bottom of the bottle is your pelvis and hips, and the top is your head. As you breathe in, picture the air as pure energy gradually filling up the decanter. Hold the energy for a few seconds and then see it slowly pouring out as you exhale.

The hammock

Imagine you have been walking along a beach for hours. You are very tired. Suddenly you spot a hammock at the top of a steep sand dune. You begin to climb the dune, but you are now becoming exhausted. *Only ten more steps to go, now nine* ... you can hardly stand up ... *now eight, seven, six* ... feel the agony of each step upwards ... *four, three* ... not far now ... *two, one*, you make it. Collapse into the hammock and relax completely.

The stairway

As you sit in your chair, pick a spot on the wall, slightly above your eye level, and stare at it. Do not allow your attention to waver. Take three long breaths, with normal breathing for about ten seconds between each of them. Each time you exhale think the word 'relax', and let every muscle and nerve in your body go loose and limp. After you have said 'relax' for the third time, close your eyes. Imagine you are at the top of a stairway. At the bottom of the stairs is complete relaxation. Visualise yourself descending. With each step you will become more and more relaxed. *20*, deeper in relaxation; *19* deeper; *18* deeper; and so on down to *1*. At that point you should be completely relaxed.

Meditation of the bubble

Picture yourself sitting quietly and comfortably at the bottom of a clear lake. Every time you have a negative thought, imagine it inside a bubble which gently rises out of your vision towards the surface. Then calmly wait for your next thought. If it is negative, watch it slowly rise towards the surface in another bubble. If you prefer, visualise yourself sitting next to a campfire with all your negative words and images rising in puffs of smoke, or sitting on the bank of a river with all your tension, fears and anxieties inside logs which are gently floating away from you.

Your favourite place

Visualise your favourite place – real or imagined: past, present or future. This is your very own secret place; and because it is in your mind, no one else need ever know about it. Perhaps it is in a beautiful valley with a gently flowing stream; or perhaps it is in a spaceship travelling to Mars. It is entirely up to you. Use all your senses – *see* the blue sky, *hear* the gurgling stream, *smell* the scented flowers, *taste* the cool water, *touch* the warm grass. Really *be there*. This idea may sound silly, but it isn't, for one simple reason – it works. Remain at your favourite place until you feel perfectly relaxed and ready to return to face the real world.

Coping during your speech

However panicky most people feel before making a speech, their nerves will almost certainly evaporate once they are introduced and they begin to speak. Think about it this way: most footballers feel nervous, especially before a big game. But once they hear the shrill of the first whistle, their nerves seem to disappear. The reason? At that moment all their pent-up tension is released and they can finally get on with the job in hand.

But if you do still feel nervous, here are a few top tips to help you cope.

- As you begin your speech, smile naturally, find a few friendly faces and maintain plenty of eye contact with them. As your confidence grows, look more and more at other people around the rest of the room.

- Ninety per cent of our nervousness is internal; only 10 per cent displays itself to the outside world. Unless you tell them you are nervous they won't know. So *never* tell them.

- If you begin to shake, concentrate on your knees. Try to shift the shaking down to your kneecaps. You will find that most of it will evaporate en route. Whatever does arrive there will be hidden behind the table.

- Keep your cue cards on the table so they can't rattle or end up all over the floor.

- Don't draw attention to your hands.

- Be aware of any possibly annoying personal habit you may have – such as swaying – and make a positive effort to control it.

- If your mouth becomes dry and your throat tightens up, the obvious thing to do is to take a sip of water. But if this isn't possible, imagine you are sucking an orange.

However, always remember that the greatest antidotes to nerves are *preparation* and *attitude*. If you prepare well and have a positive attitude, what used to be called fear can be renamed excitement and anticipation.

4 Rehearsing and Delivering Your Speech

This chapter is not about rehearsing and delivering *a* speech; it is about rehearsing and delivering *your* speech. You may want some advice on improving your voice skills, or perhaps in projecting more positive body language. Then again, you may be considering including some props as you speak. In any or all of these eventualities, you'll find all the top tips and suggestions you'll ever need.

However, this chapter is also about presenting your material in such a way that your unique personality shines through. Did Elvis, Sinatra and Johnny Rotten all sound the same singing *My Way*? Of course not. The artist makes the crucial difference. So, too, does the speaker.

Rehearsing your speech

Why do some actors freeze or fumble on the opening night and then pick up a drama award a few months later? It's a fear of unfamiliarity. As the days, weeks and months go by, the fear abates and the quality of the performance improves.

Words become more familiar. Awkward juxtapositions are smoothed out. You suddenly think of a way of saying a stuffy sentence in a more straightforward and conversational style. At the same time, you will recognise the parts of your speech that hit the spot, the parts that require a little fine tuning, and the parts that are simply not worth including.

Friends who tell you not to worry should worry you. It will *not* be alright on the night if you're under-prepared and under-rehearsed. And it's so much easier – and so much more fun – both for you and your audience, when you know exactly what you're doing.

As with the type of script you use, so the rehearsal method must be the one that best suits you. Some speakers like to be isolated and unheard in a distant room, with or without a mirror or camcorder. Others perform their speeches again and again to a sympathetic spouse or friend, either encouraging suggestions from them, or requiring nothing more than a repeated hearing to ease away inhibitions.

No one can tell you how many times you need to rehearse your speech. However, the best advice is: rehearse it until you feel you couldn't do it any better without the audience being there.

Finding your style

Every speaker is unique; every speaker has a unique style. What might be most effective for one person would be a disaster for another. It is therefore exceedingly difficult to discuss style and technique in general terms, since the ability to 'hold an audience', to be entertaining, relevant and amusing is such a personal business. However, there are certain 'rules' and guidelines which appear to be universal. Here they are.

Making the speech 'yours'

Whatever individual characteristics you have that are special to you should be nurtured and cultivated and worked on, for it is those personal and unique quirks of appearance, personality and expression that will mark you out as a speaker with something different to offer. And that is never a bad thing.

Being passionate

What makes the difference between a speech that is remembered and one that has great content but is soon forgotten? It is the passion, purpose and personality that make the difference. You do not need to be an erudite, charismatic orator – although that helps – but you *do* need to display genuine conviction, devotion – and love.

Connecting with your audience

The writer E.M. Forster's mantra was: 'Only connect'. There is a huge difference between impressing an audience and connecting with them. The guests must be certain that you are sharing your innermost feelings – that you feel the truth of the subject, physically, emotionally, spiritually. They need to know you are breaking through clichés and moving into profound territory.

The ultimate connection is when you make each of them feel you are speaking just to them. In a vicarious way, they share *your* emotions, *your* memories, *your* experiences. At the same time, they silently contemplate *their* related emotions, *their* memories, *their* experiences.

The subject has become larger than itself. It has become a window into our world, an excuse for reflecting upon the most significant matters of the human experience. A bridge has been built; a bond forged. It is a wonderful feeling because an invisible chain now links every person in the room, regardless of age, gender, race, background or creed.

Using your voice well

If you are not used to speaking in public, you will find it useful to first assess your current speaking skills and make any improvements necessary to turn yourself into a polished public speaker.

Your voice is the main means of communicating with your audience and your aim must always be to speak fluently, intelligibly, animatedly and with confidence in order to convey genuine:

- joy and ease;
- sincerity;
- enthusiasm.

Your joy and ease will make your audience feel comfortable. Your sincerity will convince them you mean every word you say. And your enthusiasm will be infectious.

So how well do you speak? Do you speak loudly enough? Do you vary your pitch and tone? Do you pronounce each word correctly and distinctly? You probably don't know because you never listen to yourself. To be an effective communicator, you *must* listen to your own voice and practise different ways of getting your message across. For this reason it would be useful to get hold of a camcorder or at least a dictaphone before you proceed.

Assessing your current skills

Every speaker needs those basic abilities which hold and retain an audience's attention. The key to avoiding tedium is variety: pace, style, pitch and tone. Try to inject a sparkle into your speech. Emphasize your main points. Convey the true meaning of your words. Express your deepest feelings.

This useful tip comes from actor David Suchet:

> *Imagine that your audience is blind. They cannot see you. Because you will have to get into their ears, the energy in your voice will change and grow immediately. It will happen subconsciously. It will make you speak very differently.*

The best way to find out how well you speak is to make an objective evaluation of your current performance. Read your speech through a number of times until you are familiar and comfortable with it. Then record yourself presenting it. Finally, play the recording back and assess yourself against these guidelines:

- speed;
- pausing;
- articulation;
- enunciation;
- pronunciation;
- modulation;
- repetition;
- projection.

Improving your speaking skills

Don't worry about technical words like 'articulation', 'enunciation' and 'modulation'. As we shall now see, the words may be difficult but the concepts are quite straightforward.

Speed

Time yourself presenting the speech. You will need to talk more slowly than you do normally. This allows your audience to absorb and consider what you are saying – and have plenty of time to laugh at all your hilarious jokes!

Try to aim at about 100 words per minute (wpm). This is a little slower than you should speak on the Big Day, but the flow of adrenaline you will experience when you stand and deliver will speed you up to the right speed (about 130 wpm). If you rehearse at this speed, you'll probably speed up to around 160 wpm, which is too fast.

Pausing

Have you punctuated your speech with short pauses? Here are a few possible examples:

Reverend Green, Ladies and Gentlemen – [pause] *Friends...*

But let's face it, [bride] *is a very lucky lady too.* [pause] *No, I don't mean ...*

Talking of words, do you know what the name [groom's first name] *actually means?* [pause] *Well, believe it or not ...*

A pause can create anticipation in an audience, and heighten its attention for whatever follows. It can be used to good effect:

- before you start;
- before an important phrase or sentence, or perhaps mid-sentence;
- before a change in style, such as humour to seriousness;
- before your close;
- before your toast;
- before you sit down.

Articulation

This means speaking distinctly. Listen to your recording once again. Did you speak clearly? Did you say 'Ladies and Gentlemen' or 'Ladiesangentlemen'? If you need to improve your articulation, try:

- moving your lips more than you would normally;
- emphasising the consonants slightly more;
- leaving a very short pause between each word.

Enunciation

Did you emphasise key words, syllables and phrases?

The best way to get the last word in any argument is to say 'sorry'.

This is the happiest day in my life ... the happiest day so far *that is ...*

We all do this in everyday conversation, but it is a good idea to exaggerate

51

slightly more when giving a speech. It adds variety, as well as bringing out important points.

Pronunciation

Were you able to pronounce every word correctly?

Poor pronunciation makes a bad impression and may confuse your audience. If you have any doubts, use an alternative expression. There are plenty of other suitable words or phrases you can substitute that you *can* pronounce.

Modulation

How much did you vary your pitch, tone and volume? Modulation is essential to keep your audience's interest and to guide them through your points. Most of us modulate naturally throughout routine conversations, but some people sink into a monotone when making a speech. If your delivery sounded a little flat, listen to a variety of TV and radio presenters. Notice how they use modulation to introduce a new topic, break up points, convey whether comments are serious or light-hearted, and so on.

Nervousness raises the pitch of the voice. So, when starting your speech, your voice is likely to be higher than normal. You should deliberately lower your voice a little to compensate. If you *think* about your words as you speak, your pitch will vary automatically.

Repetition

While this is generally to be avoided in written work, it can be used to great effect in a speech. When repeating words or phrases, it is best to vary the tone and pitch, for example:

We will have a wonderful life – a wonderful *life together.*

Projection

The last – and most important – question is: Will everyone be able to hear you? If not, all else is lost. If you need to improve your projection, stand up straight, and take two or three deep breaths. Then start speaking, concentrating on throwing your voice (but not shouting). Practise until you can project your voice with ease.

Here are some hints that will help you project your voice more effectively.

- Keep your head up.
- Open your mouth more than during normal speech.
- Use clear consonants.
- Speak more slowly than usual.

Once you have assessed your current speaking skills, work on any areas where you have identified potential for improvement. Then record yourself again. Are you now satisfied with your delivery? Continue this process until you are. A speech is like a pair of shoes – it will always benefit from a little more polishing.

Using a microphone?

There is no denying a microphone can add instant power and authority to your voice. However, a microphone is merely a tool to amplify it, not a substitute for good vocal expression. It won't make a boring voice interesting – just louder.

Doing a sound check

In some situations, a technician may set up the sound system and actively control the levels while you speak. If there is no professional available to assist you, ask a friend to act as your audience, moving around the room to evaluate sound volume and quality. Test for the levels that fill the room with sound.

Then go slightly louder to compensate for the murmuring and rustling of an actual audience.

Mic technique

Find out precisely how the microphone works and then try to get some practice. When you stand up, calmly pick it up and hold it still, just below your chin, not against your mouth – unless the wedding theme is *Star Wars* and you want to sound like Darth Vader. Make sure it's comfortable, that it doesn't obscure too much of your face and, most importantly, that you can be clearly heard. You still have to use your full voice to engage your audience and establish your identity as a speaker.

Under the pressure of speaking to an audience, a speaker can lose natural vocal expression. Be aware of that risk and guard against it. As you rehearse, experiment with volume, pitch and rhythm to achieve optimal expression and emphasis. By varying each of these, you'll be able to convey meaning and emotion. Without variation, your voice will sound boring and monotonous.

Watching your (body) language

When considering wedding speeches, many people concentrate solely on the spoken word. They forget that their unspoken physical messages – their body language – will also have a major impact. An audience does a lot more than just listen to a speech – it *experiences* it. Everything about a speaker's manner and demeanour contributes to the overall impression and feeling an audience takes away. Body language is potent. We *speak* with our vocal cords, but we *communicate* with our whole body.

All the main elements of body language – stance and posture, movement and gestures, and eye contact and facial expression – are immediately related and interdependent. You must send out an overall co-ordinated non-verbal message. And this message must also be consistent with your verbal message or you will lose all credibility. In the words of the old Chinese proverb: Watch out for the man whose stomach does not move when he laughs.

It is not possible to successfully fake body language, but it is possible to learn how to project yourself far more positively, thereby showing your audience that you are:

- sincere;
- enthusiastic;
- natural;
- friendly;
- and proficient.

What hidden messages do you give out when you speak? If you are unsure, record yourself as you rehearse, watch yourself in a mirror, or ask a kind but critical friend to comment. You may find that you need to work on one or more of the following:

- stance and posture;
- movement and gestures;
- eye contact and facial expression.

However, remember that while each of these may be considered in isolation, a change made to any one of them will also have a direct and immediate effect on the others.

Conveying confidence and integrity

Your stance and posture are important. You are making a fundamental statement with your body. An aligned, upright posture conveys a message of confidence and integrity.

Early man frightened his enemies by inflating his chest and spreading his arms to present a much wider profile (see Figure 1). Modern man uses exactly the same technique, consciously or unconsciously, when he wants to convince others of his dominance (see Figure 2).

Fig. 1. The caveman's aggressive body language

This domineering stance is
unsuitable for making a
wedding speech

A friendly, upright, open,
unthreatening stance is far
preferable

Fig. 2. Don't threaten the guests!

Standing correctly

Stand upright with your feet shoulder-width apart and very slightly turned out. You can then shift your weight from one side to the other, if you have to, without being noticed. Keep well clear of the table; leaning on it would make you look aggressive, and you could end up crying over spilt champagne. Don't put your hands in your pockets or grasp them together unnaturally at your back or front. If you are using a script or cue cards, either hold them in one hand or place them on the table in front of you. This allows you to glance at them from time to time while still giving you the freedom to use your hands to help express yourself.

Don't shield yourself

Our instincts tell us that anyone who shields himself – even with just his arms – is being defensive; while anyone who does not shield himself is perceived as friendly (see Figures 3 and 4).

Fig. 3. Early man used a shield to defend himself.

Closed arms are seen as
defensive and negative

Open arms and open palms are
considered friendly and positive

Fig. 4. Don't defend yourself against the guests!

Reinforcing your verbal messages

You should be far more than just a talking head. You don't want to be so motionless that you look like a statue on loan from Madame Tussaud's. But, equally, you shouldn't attempt an impersonation of John McCririck's Saturday afternoon arm-waving histrionics. It is perfectly possible to make simple hand gestures which reinforce your verbal messages without distracting your audience.

Avoiding hostile gestures

Early man attacked his victims by holding a weapon above their heads and bringing it down with great force (see Figure 5). Our legacy from this is that, even today, our ancestral memories perceive similar positions and movements as extremely hostile (see Figure 6). Avoid any gestures that are likely to be seen as negative or inappropriate.

Fig. 5. The hostile caveman.

Hands and fingers pointing
upwards and finger-wagging
sweeping movements are
seen as threatening

Open palms with fingers
downward are seen as
unthreatening and friendly

Fig. 6. Don't be hostile to the guests!

Practising your gestures

When you begin your speech you may feel more at ease if you keep your elbows at your sides with your hands held lightly in front of you. Once you get underway you will relax and your hand gestures will come naturally. As you gesture, your shoulders and head will adopt the appropriate position automatically. All your gestures should be clear, consistent and definitive. Most of all, they should be spontaneous – from within you – otherwise you will come over as robotic and insincere.

Being sincere

Movement and gesture give additional meaning to your words and add variety to your performance. However, there must always be good reasons for them or they will become no more than distractions. Worse still, if they are not consistent with your verbal message and the rest of your body language, your credibility will be brought into question.

Identifying your bad habits

Most of us would readily admit to having at least one habit or gesture we would prefer to lose. So, once again, it is well worth recording yourself, having a critical look into a mirror, or asking a friend to comment. Do any of these faults apply to you?

- Playing with your watch.
- Talking with your hand in front of your mouth.
- Pushing your glasses back up your nose.
- Jingling coins in your pocket.
- Waving your hands about for no reason.
- Rustling your notes.
- Shuffling your feet.
- Making pointless gestures.
- Swaying.

Try to eliminate any such habits because they are a powerful means of distraction. Your audience will become preoccupied with your mannerisms and will start watching out for them rather than experiencing your speech.

Using your head

Eye contact and facial expression are crucial aspects of effective communication because they gain and then maintain an audience's attention, create rapport, and give you valuable feedback as to how well you are coming across. The worst thing you can do, apart from mumbling inaudibly, is not to *look* at your audience. You should have memorised your opening and closing lines, so look at your audience as you deliver them. During the middle section of your speech try to keep your head up from your script or cue cards for at least 90 per cent of the time.

Maintaining eye contact

Look at everyone in the room and make this deliberate and noticeable. Stop occasionally to look at individuals for just long enough to give the impression that you are talking to them without picking them out for special attention – unless, of course, you *are* talking specifically to or about them.

Smiling

There is nothing more captivating than a smile. It shows warmth and friendliness and says: 'I'm delighted to be here giving this speech. It's going to be great fun and we're all going to have a wonderful time!' So smile, smile – and then smile (see Figure 7).

Fig. 7. Smile, smile and smile again!

Captivating your audience

The effectiveness of your speech will depend, to a large extent, on how you look and sound. Relaxed stance and upright posture, purposeful economy of movement and fluid gestures, lively eyes and facial expression, and expressive voice, will all capture your audience's attention and greatly enhance the power of your message.

Using props

In public speaking, the term 'prop' is a shortened version of the theatrical term 'property', a word used to describe any object handled or used by an actor in a performance. As a speaker you are a performer. You therefore have the right – indeed the duty – to use whatever means are necessary and available to be entertaining and to help you get your message across to the audience.

Props are really useful because they add interest and variety to your speech, focusing attention on the points you are making verbally. They also make far better connections than words with the visually oriented members of your audience.

In the beginning was the prop

The use of props can also be a great way to ease a nervous speaker into his or her speech. If you are known to be a little wordy, uncover and invert a massive egg-timer, or bring on reams of printer paper before discarding them, to the audible relief of the guests. If you're known to be quite an emotional person, why not begin by throwing packets of tissues into the crowd?

Memories are made of this

Memorability is another great reason to use props. People remember pictures far longer than words. That's also why it's so important for speakers to paint word pictures that create images in the audience's mind. These images will be remembered when the words are long forgotten. If you're not a great storyteller, you can use props to help create these mental pictures.

Effective and sensible use of props can really spice up your speech, so long as you don't hide behind them. By including music, slides, film or other aids during your speech, you will underline everything you say with great impact. People won't be expecting it and will appreciate the extra effort. Your speech will be funnier, more emotional, punchier and all the more memorable for it.

Visiting the venue

If you are considering using props, especially of a more technical nature, try to visit the venue before the Big Day. Find out how much space you'll have and what props or facilities you could use. Are there enough plug sockets? Do they have their own TV screen or projector? Is there an effective public address system? Think about what would work in this particular room. Ask questions and then judge for yourself.

Picture this

If you have access to a projector, you could show a few minutes' footage – preferably with commentary or music. Do you have any old recordings or home videos? If you do, you won't need to be a Spielberg or Scorsese to cut together your favourite moments of magic and mirth, or to get someone to do so professionally. It's so worthwhile because the rewards will be massive.

A simple PowerPoint presentation can also be used to great effect. Pick a dozen or so images and tell a short, simple story, as the pictures flick by. It's original and eye-opening and will provide a visual impact to whatever you say. Add poignant or humorous music to go with them and the audience will be absorbed. Another possibility would be to create a montage of perhaps 20 to 30 photographs, covering your subject's childhood, adolescence, hobbies, holidays and so on. Leave it projected as a backdrop as you speak. It's another sure-fire winner.

Personal possessions

Have a bag or box under the table filled with embarrassing personal artefacts: his Right Said Fred T-shirt; her Bros record collection; their school reports. Use anything amusing and incriminating from the past to add a visual impact to your stories.

Fun and games

Playing a speech game is a great way of getting the whole audience involved. If possible, try to devise you own activity, maybe relating to the couple's interests or hobbies. In this way, you will be original and creative. However, if you can't come up with any ideas, here are a few fallback possibilities.

The sweepstake game

Everyone guesses the duration of the best man's speech. The person who makes the closest estimate wins a bottle of bubbly, or something similar.

The limerick game

Put a note on all the tables asking the guests to make up a clean limerick or short poem about the couple. The best man reads out the best ones during his speech. Alternatively, ask people to read out their own contributions.

True or false?

The best man invites everyone to stand up – if they are able – and asks them a 'silly question' about the bride ('True or false: her favourite colour is pink?'). He tells them to wave their right arm in the air if it's true or to put their fingers in their ears if it's false (or something equally ridiculous). Then he asks the bride to say whether it is true or false. Those who were correct remain standing while the others are asked to sit down.

He then asks another 'impossible' true–false question, but this time about the groom. Again, he gets them to indicate their answers in some ludicrous way. The groom gives the correct response and more guests are eliminated. Then it's back to a question about the bride. The process continues until we have an overall winner.

Practice makes perfect

Before the Big Day, run through everything you intend to say and do – if possible, at the actual venue. Keep rehearsing until you are totally happy with every aspect of your speech. A champion sportsman, after yet another successful day at the office, was accused of being no more than a lucky so-and-so. He laughed politely and calmly responded: 'You know, the more I practise, the luckier I seem to become.' It is the same with speakers: the more you practise, the luckier – and the better – you are certain to become. Practice really does make perfect.

5 Making the Father of the Bride's Speech

A great wedding speech is always personal, genuine and one hundred per cent heartfelt. The degree of emotion conveyed and the style and tone you adopt must be your decision based upon many unique factors and influences, including your personality, your daughter's personality and the relationship that exists between the two of you. If you feel uncomfortable saying something, don't say it.

While it's entirely up to you how you decide to play it, the important thing is that your speech should give the entire proceedings a human quality and dimension. Get it right and it will add a special touch to your daughter's day that money simply cannot buy.

Getting the etiquette right

As Rowan Atkinson put it in his famous comedy sketch: 'There comes a time in every wedding reception when the man who paid for the damn thing is allowed to speak a word or two of his own.' And in days gone by, there often appeared to be a direct correlation between the length of his contribution and the amount of money he had forked out.

Today it is the exception rather than the rule for the father of the bride to fund the entire event, yet it remains the norm for him to speak first. And traditionally he would be expected to include the following broad sections and messages in his speech.

- Hook your audience, introduce yourself and officially welcome guests on behalf of your family.

- Give a special mention of any close friends or family who were unable to attend.

- Thank everyone involved in the organisation (and funding).

- Express your pride in your daughter.

- Welcome your son-in-law into the family.

- Welcome his family.

- Reminisce about your daughter's pre-wedding years.

- Pay a tribute to the bride's mother (whether or not you are [still] married to her).

- Proffer some personalised advice to the couple.

- Wish them success and happiness for the future.

- Propose a toast to the bride and groom.

You may well decide to follow this time-honoured format. However, with so many social and demographic changes over recent years, perhaps one or more of these traditional sections and messages may seem inappropriate to you. Or maybe given the happy couple's families' circumstances and backgrounds, you may wish to add something completely new.

In a fairly informal setting, you could simply thank everyone for coming and then propose a toast. However, your daughter may feel a little short-changed by this minimalist approach. As it's her big day, it is better to at least:

- Thank everyone involved in the organization (and funding).

- Speak proudly of your daughter and welcome her new husband into your family.

- Thank everyone for coming.

- Propose a toast to the bride and groom.

Acting as the warm-up man?

If you are quite nervous about making your speech, a good ploy is to suggest that the groom or best man will soon be 'entertaining us' or 'treating us to their words of wit and wisdom'. This creates an air of expectation and anticipation among the guests, and, to some extent at least, takes the pressure off you by implying that 'the best is yet to come'.

Seizing the moment

So while it is perfectly possible to say everything you want to in just a couple of minutes, you may decide to take this golden opportunity to make a longer, more thoughtful public tribute to your daughter (and her mother). Don't hold back the urge to tell your daughter that you're so proud of the woman she's become and that you are truly delighted for her. She may already know this, but she needs to hear it from her dad.

A warm speech, full of memories, light anecdotes and gentle humour is certain to make your guests feel connected and contented. The emotion and humour you convey can be intensified by showing a short film or some early-years photos of your daughter as you speak. Get it right and she'll treasure the memory – and possibly the DVD – for years to come.

Making it unique and memorable

Great speeches come from the heart. Every father is different; every father and daughter relationship is different; every extended family dynamic is different. Precisely what you say and how you say it will be affected by these and other factors. However, regardless of your personal circumstances and the degree of formality of the wedding, it is undeniably true that this is a massive day in your daughter's life and your speech should reflect this. Tone is everything. A warm and heartfelt speech will offend nobody and win over everybody.

Clearly the focus of your speech must be your beloved daughter. One or two well-chosen anecdotes which illustrate your strong personal feelings will be far more effective and memorable than a whole series of half-hearted passing references to the pleasure and delight you are experiencing on this most happy of days. Choose stories that have a telling point about her personality, ones that will have a positive effect on the audience and will stick in their memories.

Many of the most memorable father of the bride speeches were written with a common theme in mind: perhaps how the bride has continually overcome hardships and struggles, or maybe by providing a nostalgic picture of how she has developed from a stroppy youth to sensible young woman. A great speech will always incorporate many different thoughts and emotions, but they will all be connected under one overarching theme.

You may already have a pretty good idea of the theme you are going to develop and incidents you are going to describe to support it. If not, the best way to recall some poignant and illuminating episodes is to think about one or two of these memory joggers:

- Birthdays.
- Turning points.
- Major decisions.
- School.
- College.
- First job.
- Illness.
- Influential people.
- Holidays.
- Christmas.
- Friends.
- Hobbies.
- Ambitions.
- Games and toys.
- Pets.
- Travel.

Pour yourself a drink, take a hot bath or go for a long walk and the memories will come flooding back. Better still, sleep on it. You really will get some of your best ideas this way. Your subconscious mind will take over and come up with a whole series of interesting and often unexpected memories and connections.

Papa don't preach

The perfect father of the bride speech has the following qualities.

Optimism

This is not the time to share your personal woes, paint a gloomy picture of the present or offer dire predictions about the future. Stress your certainty that in her husband's care, your daughter will prosper along with him and – with a little homily on the 'give and take' necessary to a successful marriage – the confidence you have that happiness must accompany the love they so evidently bear for one another.

A tribute to the happy couple

Refer to some positive characteristics of both the bride and groom that are well known to the audience (perhaps speak of your 'devoted daughter' and her 'hard-working husband'). Then declare your confidence that they will make all the effort needed and will not be found wanting. This is a marriage made in heaven. They were made for each other.

Emotional impact

You should feel free to display strong personal feelings. Describe an incident or two that demonstrate the joy you and your partner have had bringing up your daughter. But be wary: too much schmaltz can unbalance things. Use sincerity and emotion with caution and constraint. Gauge what most warm, right-thinking people would regard as a justifiable level of love and pride.

If you feel you simply must let the world know how totally elated you are feeling, divert some of your emotional outpourings away from your daughter and towards the bride's mother, the groom and to the pleasure you have found in getting to know him – and his family. However, never fake it; you must always be one hundred per cent genuine in everything you say.

Conveying emotion

Far too many fathers make the mistake of dwelling on their own feelings and reactions and can be stunned and crestfallen to discover that no one else in the room can relate to their genuine sentiments and fail to respond to their proud, misty-eyed recitation of their daughter's every achievement, from a gold star at nursery for creating something or other with egg boxes, to her university degree. 'But I was almost in tears as I was saying this,' they protest. 'How could the guests not be similarly moved?' How indeed?

Emotions are abstract concepts

The problem is that our feelings are abstract. It is not that we do not hear or understand abstractions, but without a visual peg, without something we can conjure in our minds with colour and form, intangible ideas and concepts make little impact and are soon forgotten.

Talk about the incident, not the emotion

The best way to convey your feelings is to focus upon an incident which illustrates them. Concentrate, not upon the emotion that was evoked, but on the situation which gave rise to it. Turn abstract ideas into strong, concrete mental images. What you must do is to take each guest by the hand and guide them through your valley of emotions without ever having to mention any of those emotions by name.

Don't bore the audience with long introductions or unnecessary explanation. Get straight to the heart of the matter. Focus on a single incident or situation; providing a snapshot that it will remain alive in their minds and hearts. The more apparently mundane and ordinary the circumstances surrounding the occasion, the more powerful and extraordinary will be the emotion it evokes.

I keep all my important certificates and awards in a drawer in the living room – my 1975 BSc, my 1983 accountancy qualification, my 2009

Salesman of the Year award. But shall I tell you which certificate I treasure most? Compared to this one all the others pale into insignificance. I won it back in 1992; well actually I won it jointly. You can keep the BSc, the ACA and the Salesman of the Year . . . my most treasured award is the one for first place in the 1992 [daughter's school] *father and daughter egg and spoon race. That award means more to me than a Nobel Prize or an Oscar. We were a real team that day. And,* [daughter], *I want you to know that you'll always be in first place in my heart.*

Everything you say needs to be thoughtful and unique, a loving reminder that our imperfections are part of our charm, and the sentiments of love, family and friendship shared together on this day are the truly important wedding accessories.

Saying it with humour

However, people can only take so much emotion. The way to avoid guests overdosing is to enliven and intermix your sentimental reminiscences with gentle touches of humour. You need to offer a mixture of material that will at one moment tug at the heartstrings and at the next have them laughing in the aisles.

Looking into the mirror

Any speaker who cannot laugh at himself leaves the job to others. Poke a little fun at yourself before you poke fun at anyone else.

What a panic yesterday evening. I heard [daughter] *say to her mother, 'Mum, I've still got so much to do and I want everything to be perfect. I'm determined not to overlook even the most insignificant detail.' And her mother replied, 'Don't worry, love, I'll make sure your father is there.'*

Your daughter

Don't forget that it's her Big Day. And a few indelicate words can shatter it. Target any humour with extreme caution and care. Does she have a good sense of humour? If she's game for a laugh, then she's fair game.

[Daughter] *had their joint credit card stolen last month.* [Son-in-law] *hasn't reported it as missing because the thief is taking less out each week than she was.*

Your son-in-law

Once again, don't be too cruel and consider how he – and his family – is likely to react to a little gentle ribbing.

In many ways [son-in-law] *has become like a son to me. He doesn't take any notice of what I say, he's always answering back and he is threatening to eat us out of house and home.*

Your wife

Target a mild potshot in this direction only if you are sure it will be received by your good lady in the humorous spirit that you no doubt intended.

Being a romantic sort of girl, [wife] *insisted on getting married in her grandmother's dress. She looked absolutely fabulous – but her poor old granny nearly froze to death.*

Be positively insulting

Funnily enough, a teasing jibe and a sincere compliment often fit well together, each reinforcing the other in a kind of verbal synergy. The trick is to first set up a situation which you can exploit with a teasing remark, before turning this into a genuine compliment.

When she was 16, [daughter] *joined the string section of the town orchestra. She practised at home day and night. For years she was always harping on about something or other . . . Well, angels do, don't they?*

If an anecdote is funny, try to blend in a little poignancy. Conversely, if it's emotionally stirring, add a touch of humour.

Offering some words of wisdom

Rather than simply regurgitating the same old, clichéd pearl or trinket of wisdom that has been heard by a million other couples, try to personalise any advice you may wish to offer. Give the bride and groom (and everyone else in the room) the benefit of any relevant life lessons you have learned through success or failure. How can they apply this to their lives?

Now it is customary on an occasion such as this for the father of the bride to pass on some words of wisdom about love and marriage. Well, just before I got married back in 1978, my father gave us some invaluable advice which I now pass on to you two today. Dad produced a large sheet of white paper just like this one [hold up a sheet of paper] *and drew a tiny black dot in the centre* [do the same]. *'What do you see?' he asked. 'A little spot,' we replied. 'Anything else?' We looked hard at the paper and then at each other with blank expressions. 'You see a little black dot which represents the problems that you may face in the future. What you have both missed is all the white space that makes up the rest of the page. Good things can easily be ignored and taken for granted simply because they are so obvious. Always look beyond any tiny black spots and appreciate that huge white space.'*

Including some winning lines

The following selection provides a miscellany of openers, jokes, one-liners, quotations and toasts which you could use, or adapt and personalise, to suit the precise circumstances of the wedding.

Opening lines

Ladies and Gentlemen, it has been said that love is the light and sunshine of life. We cannot enjoy ourselves, or anything else, unless someone we love enjoys it with us. Well, from this day forth Emily and Derek will be enjoying their lives together.

Ladies and Gentlemen, 'Love has the magic power to make a beggar a king.' I wish I'd have said that . . . come to think of it, I just did.

Ladies and Gentlemen, my dad taught me always to remember the ABC and the XYZ of speechmaking. ABC: Always be concise. XYZ: Examine your zip [look down].

Good ladies, afternoon and Gentlemen . . . I **knew** *I should have rehearsed this speech.*

Ladies and Gentlemen, I won't be speaking for very long . . . This suit has to be back in twenty minutes.

Ladies and Gentlemen, unaccustomed as I am to public speaking, I feel this irresistible urge to prove it.

A touch of humour

Ideally, you will be as wry as you are romantic – as witty as you are wise – as you incorporate some more light-hearted musings into your speech. However, a word of warning: by all means include some gentle humour, but do so with extreme care. Don't shatter your daughter's big day by delivering a thoughtless line. To say: 'Marriage isn't a word, it's a sentence' is a great line for a stand-up comedian, but it has absolutely no place in a wedding speech.

I'm not losing a daughter; I'm gaining a bathroom.

I'm delighted to be here today. Mind you, at my age, I'm delighted to be anywhere.

When Katie was in one of her disobedient moods her mother told her to behave herself. 'I will for a fiver,' replied Katie. 'You shouldn't ask for money to be good,' Lynne said. 'You should be good for nothing – just like your father.'

Some people ask the secret of our long marriage. We take time to go out to a restaurant two times a week. A little candlelight, dinner, soft music and dancing. She goes Tuesdays, I go Fridays.

I asked my wife if she remembered our wedding night. 'Reg,' she said, 'that was 33 years ago, there's no need to apologise now.'

I shall never forget my marriage because I had to ask my wife's mother permission to marry her daughter. 'Have you the means to make her happy?' she asked. 'Well,' I said, 'it'll make her laugh and I'm afraid that's the best I can do.'

Any man who thinks he is smarter than his wife is married to a very smart woman.

Quotations

Including a quotation or two can really lift a speech, especially if they encapsulate your thoughts and feelings. Guests will appreciate hearing the perceptive words of others. However, don't overdo it. For most of the time they would much prefer to share *your* innermost sentiments and reflections, not someone else's.

Live so that when your children think of fairness, caring and integrity, they think of you. (H. Jackson Brown, Jr)

Love is the light and sunshine of life. We cannot fully enjoy ourselves, or anything else, unless someone we love enjoys it with us. (Sir John Avebury)

Marriage is three parts love and seven parts forgiveness. (Langdon Mitchell)

There is only one happiness in life: to love and be loved. (George Sand)

The most important thing a father can do for his children is to love their mother. (Theodore Hesburgh)

Immature love says: 'I love you because I need you';
Mature love says: 'I need you because I love you.' (Confucius)

Toasts

The purpose of your speech is to propose a toast to the bride and groom. However, you may also wish propose a toast to people who mean or meant a lot to one or both of the newlyweds, yet are unable to be there today to celebrate their marriage. The tone of this secondary toast would depend to a large degree on the reason for their absence. It should be made fairly early on in your speech, before you return seamlessly to your central congratulatory and upbeat message. Sometimes the groom will make this toast, but most commentators counsel against this unless one or more of the couple's parents is ill or has recently died.

Similarly, it often falls upon the bride's dad to help make any children of the bride and/or groom feel genuinely welcomed and valued, although, of course, this process should have begun long before the speeches. Whether the wedding has cemented their parents' existing relationship, or perhaps marked the formation of a new family, it is extremely important for children to feel that they – indeed to *know* that they – are welcomed, embraced – and loved. However, three toasts in one speech may seem a little excessive. If the father of the bride is to raise a toast to absent friends, perhaps the bridegroom and others could propose a toast to the children. When it comes to involving and welcoming children into a family unit, you really can't overdo it.

To absent friends (from far away)

I spoke to Len and Ruby this morning. They asked me to pass on their apologies for not being able to make it here from Oz and to send you their very best wishes. They also told me they will be raising a glass to you both today, right now in fact . . . at 4 in the morning! So let's raise a glass to them, too, and to all other family and friends who couldn't join us here today. Ladies and Gentlemen, please join me in a toast to absent friends.

To absent friends (illness – not serious)

Amanda's cousin Mario phoned yesterday to say he was so sorry but he wasn't going to be able to make it here today because of his recent footballing injury. He damaged his hand last Saturday. Apparently he was watching Match of the Day *when he cut it while opening his fifth can of Stella. Anyway, let's all wish him well as we raise our glasses to him and to all other absent friends. To absent friends.*

To absent friends (illness – more serious)

Regrettably, Kiera's Aunty Jane can't be with us today because of her recent illness. She really would have loved to have seen Kiera and Tony getting married today and I know I speak on behalf of everyone in this room when I wish her a full and speedy recovery. Let's all raise our glasses and drink a toast to absent friends.

To absent friends (deceased)

Sadly, as many of you will know, Uncle Robert passed away earlier this year. Although we all miss Bob terribly, we can rejoice in the fact that he would have been absolutely delighted that Heather and Garrett have now tied the knot. In a sense I feel he is celebrating here with us today because, like me, Bob knew the two of you were just made for one another. Ladies and Gentlemen, please remain seated as we drink a toast to absent friends.

To children

You can't fool kids. They are true judges of character and they tell it like it is. That's why I'm absolutely delighted that Nancy and Arthur love Gillian as much as Gillian so clearly loves them. Nancy, Arthur, we are all delighted to welcome you into our family. You are so, so welcome. I think we should drink a toast to you, don't you? I'm afraid you'll have to be satisfied with lemonade though. Ladies and Gentlemen, let's raise a glass to two wonderful young people: To Nancy and Arthur.

To the bride and groom

Two souls with but a single thought,
Two hearts that beat as one.

As Sandra and Will start their new life,
Let us all toast the new husband and wife.

May your love be as endless as your wedding rings.

There are only two lasting bequests we can hope to give our children. One of these is roots, the other wings.

Much happiness to the newlyweds from the oldlyweds.

In the words of that old Bobby Vee hit: Take Good Care of My Baby. Ladies and gentlemen, I give you the bride and groom. [If you then play the record it will bring the house down.]

A sample speech

The important thing is to make your speech unique, personal and relevant. The following example follows the traditional father of the bride speech format. The main reason for its inclusion is to remind you of the style and tone you may wish to adopt throughout your speech.

Hook your audience, introduce yourself and officially welcome guests on behalf of your family

On a day such as this I hope I can be forgiven for indulging in a little reminiscing about the past, and perhaps making a few little predictions about the future. Today we celebrate a marriage, the union of my daughter Crystal and her new husband Lee.

Good afternoon, everyone, for those of you who do not know me, I'm Roy, Crystal's dad, and it is an honour and privilege for me to be speaking to you on this wonderful occasion. My wife Jean and I are absolutely delighted that so many of you were able to join us here. You are all very welcome.

Give a special mention of any close friends or family who were unable to attend

Sadly though, others cannot be with us and, at this point, I would like to mention a few important people who have been so influential in Crystal and Lee's lives. To begin with, my mother, Crystal's Nana Vi. She is unable to attend due to her health needs. She has doted on Crystal for 30 years. She may not be in this hall, but she is certainly in our hearts.

Then there is my father Mark who passed away last summer. He would be so proud today. And in a sense, I feel he is with us. No champagne for him though; he would have far preferred to be sipping his usual pint of bitter.

And of course we mustn't forget Lee's grandparents Albert and Gwen, who will both be looking down upon us from the stars. But they are all here in spirit, and they will all be very proud of the way the happy couple have turned out on this their most special day. Ladies and Gentlemen, please remain seated as you join me in the first toast of the day: To absent friends.

Thank everyone involved in the organisation (and funding)

Now weddings don't just happen; they take a lot of preparation and hard work. So I would like to take this opportunity to thank everyone involved. In particular, I would like express my sincere gratitude to Jean and her sisters Peggy and Norma who are sitting over there. Yes, that terrific trio really came up trumps. They have worked tirelessly over the last few months organising this reception. I know that an awful lot of time and effort have gone into the planning and I am sure you will all agree that it has been so worthwhile and that they are all to be congratulated.

Express your pride in your daughter

Well, what can I tell you about my gorgeous daughter, Crystal? She is the ultimate people person. Her priorities in life are about as selfless as it gets: friends and family always come first; then it's her job, and only finally it's herself. And, believe me, anyone who can call her friend or family is truly fortunate.

I remember her school's Sports Day back in 1990. Crystal was a really good runner and was one of the favourites to win the girls' 100 metres sprint. She was right up there with the leaders when the girl next to her fell and twisted her ankle. Crystal immediately stopped running, turned around and helped the injured girl up. She put the girl's arm over her shoulder and they slowly walked and hobbled the rest of the race together. As they both crossed the line all the spectators stood up and cheered wildly. It was a magical and memorable moment. Crystal, I admire you as much as I love you. Today I am bursting with pride. You are the daughter every parent dreams of having.

Welcome your son-in-law into the family

And what about that dashing young man sitting alongside you? Lee, one of my abiding memories of today will always be the moment you slipped the ring on my daughter's finger. You know, from the time a daughter is born, every father anticipates this happening – some with joy, others with fear.

Crystal first brought Lee home to help us celebrate our Pearl Wedding anniversary. It soon became very apparent to us that our other guests merely made a pleasant background for their love, and that for each of them there was but one other person in the room. Throughout the day we witnessed gentle looks, swift glances, silent gestures. They were both full to the brim with delicate laughter, with childlike wonder, with tranquil love. We all took a part in their gracious happiness. It was clear they were meant for each other. Lee, since I first met you, I have been anticipating that moment you slipped on the ring with uncontrollable and unconditional joy. In you, I find the perfect match for my daughter.

Lee, you will find that our family is a circle of love and strength. With every birth and every union, the circle grows. Every joy shared adds more love. Every obstacle faced together makes the circle stronger. Lee, today Jean and I are delighted to formally welcome you with open arms into our family circle.

Welcome his family

We are also honoured to welcome into our fold two other lovely people who haven't had a mention yet, but without whom Lee certainly wouldn't be here today. Of course I mean Lee's parents, Alice and Denis, already our valued friends. A warm welcome to you both.

Reminisce about your daughter's pre-wedding years

Like Jean and me, I am sure you two have a million memories of your child's wonderful growing up years. I have so many cherished memories of Crystal I could share with you here today. But the single simple memory I will treasure the most takes me back to her fifth birthday. It had been raining non-stop for over a fortnight but on her birthday, almost symbolically, it stopped. I remember seeing Crystal rush into the middle of our garden where she spread her arms wide, raised her face to the sun and span round like a top. My heart soared, seeing my little girl, how she could celebrate life, how she could take such joy out of such a simple thing as a sunny moment on a warm September's day. That memory will stay with me forever.

Crystal, you don't need a metal detector to find a real treasure. You are pure gold and it's fantastic that you've always looked towards the future with that same optimism and joy that I saw on your face that birthday afternoon. And I can see it again here right now. You're moving into your future with your arms wide open and your face turned to the light.

Pay a tribute to the bride's mother (whether or not you are [still] married to her)

You know, I really can't take full credit for the wonderful person Crystal has become. You wouldn't have grown into the loving, caring, giving individual you are today without the direction, influence and impact of your mum. Jean, I don't tell you this as often as I should, but you have been a wonderful wife and a magnificent mother and I really would like to take this opportunity to say I am the luckiest man in the world.

It's not that you do any one thing that makes you so fantastic, it's all the little things you do for us. It's the understanding and the acceptance and the way you take care of everything. It's the way you treat me, forgive me, put up with me – and love me. Lee, they say as a daughter gets older, she turns out to be more and more like her mother. If this happens to Crystal, you can ask for no more in life.

Proffer some personalised advice to the couple

Now it is customary, at this stage, for the father of the bride to offer a few words of advice to his daughter and new son-in-law, so here goes. To be honest, I didn't learn an awful lot at school. I spent most of my time avoiding work and really being a bit of a pain to my teachers. Looking back now, of course, I realise that that was very silly. But I did learn one vital life lesson which has remained with me to this day and I will now pass on my teacher's wise words of wisdom, with immense thanks, to the two of you.

It seemed like just another average sort of day. I had no reason to think it was going to be anything but another boring science lesson. How wrong I was. Our teacher stood in front of the class with a strange combination of items in front of him. He picked up a very large and empty jar and filled it with rocks, all about two inches wide. Then he asked us if the jar was full. We agreed that it was.

He then picked up a box of pebbles and poured them into the jar and shook it lightly. The pebbles rolled into the open areas between the rocks. He then asked us again if the jar was full. We agreed it was.

Next he picked up a box of sand and poured it into the jar. Of course, the sand filled up everywhere else. He asked us if the jar was now full. We responded with a unanimous 'Yes'.

He then produced two cans of beer from under the desk and poured the entire contents into the jar, effectively filling the empty space between the grains of sand. We all laughed out loud.

'Now,' said our teacher as the laughter subsided, 'I want you to recognise that this jar represents your life. The rocks are the important things – your family, your children, your health, your friends – and if everything else was lost and only they remained, your life would still be full. The pebbles are the other things that matter like your job, your house and your holidays. The sand is everything else – the trivial stuff. If you put the sand into the

jar first, there is no room for the rocks or pebbles. The same goes for life. If you spend all your time and energy on the trivial things you will never have room for the things that are important to you.

At this stage curiosity got the better of me. I raised my hand and asked what the cans represented. Our wise old teacher smiled and said, 'I'm glad you asked. The cans just shows you that no matter how full your life may seem, there's always room for a couple of beers with a friend.'

Yes, that was the most important lesson I have ever had and I like to think it has served me well throughout my life. Pay attention to the things that are critical to your happiness. Spend time with your family. Take your partner out to dinner. Walk together under the stars. There will always be times later to clean the house and mow the lawn. Concentrate on the rocks of your life first – the things that really matter. Set your priorities. The rest is just sand.

Wish them success and happiness for the future

Drawing to a close, it has been said that when you're happy, you smile, but when you're really happy your eyes smile. Well, the way Crystal and Lee have been looking at one another today, their eyes have not only been smiling, but have been absolutely beaming. So it is with great confidence that on behalf of Jean and myself, I wish you both a long, healthy and incredibly happy future together.

Propose a toast to the bride and groom.

Well it's about time all this reminiscing came to an end; it is time to move on. You know, I have come to a couple of important and inescapable conclusions here today: Jean and I have done a lot for Crystal but Crystal has done even more for us. And, Lee, there is absolutely no doubt in our minds that the time is now right to entrust her to your loving care. And knowing you, as we do, we are certain that this will be very, very good care.

Ladies and Gentlemen – Friends, please now stand and join me in a toast to the happy couple. Crystal and Lee, you have both been fortunate in finding each other – in finding your rock. May your hands be forever clasped in friendship and your hearts forever joined in love. The toast is: Crystal and Lee, bride and groom.

6 Making the Bridegroom's Speech

As if he didn't have enough to worry about on his wedding day, the bridegroom is expected to deliver a middle-of-the-road speech which is not too schmaltzy and not too biting. Also speaking on behalf of his wife, he needs to thank lots people for lots of things, while always keeping everything entertaining and amusing. Most importantly, he needs to convey his sincere feelings about his bride.

Getting the etiquette right

Traditionally, yours is the second speech, though in practice nowadays more than one other person – such as a step-parent or the mother of the bride – may also have spoken before you. You should respond to the toast proposed by the bride's father (and to anyone else who may have offered a toast to you) and later propose a toast to the bridesmaids and any other attendants. You may also wish to include a toast to your wife within your speech, but that's an optional extra.

In many ways, a bridegroom's speech can be thought of a general thank-you speech. If it moves, thank it; if it doesn't move, thank it. Thank anyone and everyone who helped make this day so special.

Of course, you will also want to talk affectionately about your new bride and tell the world – well, everyone in the room anyway – what a lucky man you are and how much you love her. Seize the opportunity to say something heartfelt. A few words about how you met and how romance blossomed, intermixed with a couple of humorous asides, would be sure to go down well. Guests always want to hear an expression of a bridegroom's love.

As always, precisely what you say, and how and when you say it, must be your choice. However, if you include the following broad sections and messages, you won't go far wrong.

- Hook your audience, introduce yourself and say you are also speaking on behalf of your wife, unless she is going to say a few words herself ('My wife and I ... ').

- Thank the bride's father for his toast, kind words and (where appropriate) enormous generosity in paying for the wedding.

- Thank anyone else (perhaps your own family) for their financial contribution.

- Thank your bride's parents for raising such a wonderful woman and for allowing you to marry her.

- Thank your parents for bringing you up to be such an upstanding citizen!

- Thank everyone for accepting their invitations to the wedding and for their wonderful gifts.

- Thank your best man, any ushers and other key helpers.

- Compliment your new wife.

- Propose a personalised toast on behalf of yourself and your bride to the bridesmaids and pageboys (unless your wife is going to speak and propose a toast to her attendants).

As a general rule, the father of the bride will raise a toast to 'absent friends'. However, if either of your or your wife's parents is ill or has recently died, you may wish to do this yourself.

Gifts

Some grooms use their speech as an opportunity to give gifts to the mothers, aunts, grandmothers, bridesmaids, ushers, the best man and so on. The problem is, if too many gifts are handed out or collected, this can seriously disrupt proceedings as the scene takes on the appearance of an unruly school prize-giving day. So unless you are giving just a couple of gifts, it is far preferable to distribute your presents and mementoes *after* the speeches.

Making it unique and memorable

You need to thank everyone involved in the organisation and funding of the wedding and be upbeat about every aspect of the day ('This wonderful occasion'; 'What a beautiful service'; 'Such a fantastic meal'; and so on). The danger here, though, is that your speech can end up sounding like a boring and self-indulgent Oscar-winning acceptance speech. The best way to avoid this happening is to lighten all your genuine compliments and words of thanks with little touches of humour:

> *My wife and I would also like to take this opportunity to thank you all for your incredibly generous gifts. I'm sure* [your wife] *will make great use of the lawn mower and I can't wait to watch her from the comfort of the new hammock.*

Turning to the bride and her family

But your speech is not merely an opportunity to thank people. You also need to address a good portion of the content to your bride and to her parents. When you speak to or about your wife, try to forget the audience for a moment, speak directly to *her* and tell her how much she means to you. But make sure everyone can hear you. There won't be a dry eye in the house.

Remember that your wife's father will (hopefully) have said what a great person you are in his speech, and will have ever so subtly told you that he expects you to look after her, for better or for worse, in sickness and in health. You therefore need to acknowledge your new father-in-law's speech and to respond to the points raised. The problem is, you may not remember precisely what he has said, so prepare a fall-back generic response that should cover pretty much any compliments he may have made:

> *Thank you for those generous words. I do not deserve the kind things you said of me, but I will try to deserve them and to be worthy of my wife.*

All good speeches should include a healthy dose of humility and compassion. Use your speech to prove to your father-in-law that you really do care. This is a very big moment for him and your bride's mum, and they will be very appreciative if the person to whom they are handing over their daughter expresses humbleness, caring and sensitivity.

Telling a few crowd-pleasers

The most entertaining speeches from grooms make reference to how they first met their bride, how their relationship developed, when they bought their first rotary clothes line and so on. Such personal revelations – both profound and mundane – hold an endless fascination for guests. By the telling of the stories, the audience gets to see 'behind the scenes' of your relationship, which like all the best television documentaries, is absolutely compelling.

Look to the future and express how excited you are about enjoying many fantastic years together. Turn to your wife and declare your undying love directly, telling it straight from the heart. By all means rehearse this, but don't read it from your notes on the day. If your wife and your guests can see that you are truly sincere, your speech is sure to be a smash hit.

Including some winning lines

Remember that light and shade in a speech make it so much more enjoyable for an audience. A sudden gearshift from wit to sentiment – and later a return to humour – works brilliantly. Here are some lines which, when suitably adapted and personalized, could merit a place within your speech.

Opening lines

Ladies and Gentlemen, my wife and I... [not a particularly funny hook but a very useful one for a bridegroom because it is guaranteed to raise howls of laughter, cheers and applause].

Ladies and Gentlemen (thank you, Bobby, for those kind words...), as Henry VIII said to each of his wives in turn, 'I shall not keep you long.'

Ladies and Gentlemen – the ladies is over there [pointing], *and the gents is over there* [pointing].

Ladies and Gentlemen, I feel like the young Arab sheik who inherited his father's harem. I know exactly what to do, but where on earth do I begin?

Ladies and Gentlemen – well, Isaac did ask me to begin with a gag.

Ladies and Gentlemen – who says flattery doesn't pay?

Ladies and Gentlemen, this is the first time I've spoken at a wedding – except during other people's speeches.

Jokes and one-liners

I'd like to thank Becky's dad for his kind words. I hope that, as Beck's husband, I can live up to the image he painted of me... or at least keep pulling the wool over his eyes.

I hope you're all enjoying yourselves on this special day. It's great to see so many friends and family here, and I can honestly say that it wouldn't be the same without you... just an awful lot cheaper.

To my new in-laws, I'd like to start by saying you're not losing a daughter ... but you are losing the chance she'll marry into money.

There are two people not yet mentioned, but without whom I wouldn't be here. No, I don't mean bar staff, but my parents, the most wonderful mum and dad in the world.

We've booked a really unusual Spanish hotel for our honeymoon ... it's finished.

I'd like to thank the Reverend Owen for the brilliant job he did today at the church. I learned something new during the vows that I hadn't realised before: that it's okay to have sixteen wives ... four better, four worse, four richer and four poorer.

I've heard a few people comment on how slim I look in this suit. This is actually the result of a fitness regime that's seen me do over 50 push-ups a day during the run-up to the wedding. But I should mention that none of them have actually been intentional ... I've just been collapsing a lot through nerves and stress.

I told Felka, 'Now we're married I want you to stick to your washing, ironing, cooking, cleaning and shopping ... No wife of mine is going to work!'

I'm so looking forward to coming home from work, opening a can, sitting on the sofa and spending the evening watching Andrea's favourite telly programmes.

I really couldn't ask for a better woman ... if I did, Michelle would kill me.

I'd like to thank Alicia for marrying me. She's the most warm, witty and wonderful woman I know. She does everything for me. She even wrote this speech.

Thanks must go to my parents for teaching me the difference between right and wrong ... so I know which I'm enjoying at any particular time.

Ricky doesn't know the meaning of the word meanness ... Mind you, he doesn't know the meaning of lots of other words either.

Jamie is such a responsible person. If there's a problem, it's odds on he's responsible.

The two of us complement each other perfectly. Victoria is ambitious and loves a challenge ... and I am that challenge.

I'll never forget the day that Jade told me I was going to marry her.

How many bridesmaids does it take to change a light bulb? Five, one to yank it out of the socket and chuck it, and four to squabble over who's going to catch it.

My best man, Simon, will be getting up to speak in a moment or two, and I can tell you he has some very unusual material, beginning with his suit.

Emotional stuff

Those of you who do not know my best man Fred are the luckiest people in the world ... that's because the pleasure of getting to know him lies ahead of you.

They say a girl grows to be like her mother; well, I can only hope it is true.

I had no ideas so many wonderful qualities could exist in one person, until I met Kayla. I really feel like the happiest man in the world.

Now I know what they write about in love songs. Mel, I've waited 28 years to feel like this and I'd like to thank you for making my life complete.

It takes two women to make a good husband – and the first one is his mother.

Tara, my lovely bride, you look more beautiful today than ever. I promise I will never stop trying to become everything you could hope for in a husband.

Today I married my best friend – the woman I laugh with, live for and dream with. Naomi, in the words of Robert Browning: 'Grow old with me, the best is yet to be.'

I've been trying to come up with something original that would sum up everything I feel about Eleri and how much she means to me. But I couldn't find the words to express what I wanted to say, so let me keep it old-fashioned and say, in the presence of our family and friends: 'Eleri, I love you.'

Toasts to the bride

And now it's time for another toast ... any excuse for a drink ... To my wife – my bride and joy.

When we're together and when we're apart,
You're first in my thoughts and first in my heart.

A ring is round, it turns forever.
And that's how long we'll be together.

Because I love you truly,
Because you love me, too,
My greatest happiness
Is sharing life with you.

A toast to my wife:
Never above you.

Never below you.
Always beside you.

Toasts to the bridesmaid(s)

I have one final duty – no, not duty, pleasure – and that is to propose a toast to the health of the bridesmaids ... Ladies and Gentlemen, the bridesmaids.

Anna and I would also like to thank our bridesmaids Pip, Georgie and Sophie who all look stunning and truly beautiful today and have added so much to our day. Thanks also to the two young men on my right, Bill and Devin. Thanks guys for all your help today. And we must not forget young Thomas who did a splendid job as pageboy. Thank you, Tom. Ladies and Gentlemen, I would like you all to stand and join me in a toast to the bridesmaids: The bridesmaids.

As Keats reminds us:
A thing of beauty is a joy forever.
Please join me in a toast to the bridesmaids...

And finally, a toast to our three lovely, helpful and charming bridesmaids. Ladies and Gentlemen ... the bridesmaids.

A sample speech

The following example has been drafted in a style and tone appropriate for a meaningful and memorable bridegroom's speech. This is a brilliant opportunity for you to reflect publicly upon the massive significance of today's events. If you follow this overall structure, you are certain not only to *meet*, but also to *exceed* the expectations of your audience.

Hook your audience, introduce yourself and say you are also speaking on behalf of your wife, unless she is going to say a few words herself ('My wife and I . . .')

Ladies and Gentlemen . . . Boys and Girls, my wife and I are absolutely delighted that you were all able to join us on this joyous day. I can't imagine a happier way to start married life than with our family and friends around us.

Now someone once said a good speech has both a good beginning and a good end. A great speech, however, keeps both of these very close together. Well I can't promise you a great speech, but I certainly intend to make it a short one, because of my throat . . . if I go on too long, Jayne has threatened to cut it. Good afternoon, everyone. I'm Alex, and quite simply, today I'm the happiest man in the world.

Thank the bride's father for his toast, kind words and (where appropriate) enormous generosity in paying for the wedding

Firstly, I want to thank Richard for those kind words you spoke about me . . . I really don't deserve them . . . but then again I have a bad back and I don't deserve that either. No, in all sincerity, I promise I will try my hardest to live up to the things you said of me. You and Margaret have been absolutely wonderful and Jayne and I would like to take this opportunity to thank you both for being so generous in helping us make this day so special.

Thank anyone else (perhaps your own family) for their financial contribution

And of course equal thanks must also go to my parents Jack and Babs for their help and support . . . and for so much more. Today has been a real joint effort. Mam and Dad, you're not losing a son . . . you're gaining an overdraft.

Thank your bride's parents for raising such a wonderful woman and for allowing you to marry her

Well, today I married my best friend, the most beautiful girl in the world and the woman I love ... I just hope they don't all meet up later. No seriously, I'd like to thank Richard and Margaret for producing Jayne and for bringing her up so fantastically well that she's turned out to be the kind, caring, considerate individual you see before you here today. You know, when I asked them for permission to marry their beautiful daughter, Richard said, 'Just leave your name and phone number and we'll be in contact if nothing better comes up.' Well I'm delighted that nothing did, and I promise I will never ever let your daughter down. I am such an incredibly lucky man.

Thank your parents for, well, bringing you up to be such an upstanding citizen!

But I suppose Jayne is lucky, too. No, not because she has married me ... though I suppose she could have done worse. No, it's because, like me, she has just gained two wonderful parents-in-law. Mam and Dad, you've always been there for me, and I know you will always be there for Jayne, too. Both Jayne and I have been so fortunate having grown up knowing the real meaning of marriage through the example of our parents.

Thank everyone for accepting their invitations to the wedding and for their wonderful gifts

*It's really brilliant that so many of you could join us here today from all over the world. Belize, Outer Mongolia and West Hartlepool are the only places **not** represented. And thank you so much for all your generous gifts. I can't tell you how much they mean to us – but I should have a far better idea after the honeymoon, once I've spoken to the guy in the pawn shop.*

Thank your best man, any ushers and other key helpers

There are so many other people to thank for making this day so memorable. Thanks to Reverend Smith for such a lovely service; her Boss for arranging this wonderful weather; the brilliant choir, cellist and organist; the bell-ringers; the caterers; the bar staff; the photographers; Allison for being such a magnificent and efficient wedding co-ordinator; Marcus, Vincent and Luke for performing their ushering duties so well and, of course, Colin for being my best man. Mind you, I'm not sure how thankful to be because I haven't heard his speech yet. If I've left anyone out, I apologise. You know who you are. Immense thanks to everyone involved.

Compliment your new wife

Now, Jayne, you thought you knew all the 'thank yous' I was going to make here today. But there's one more you didn't know about. Jayne, thank you for being my lovely bride. You can't help being lovely . . . but you could help being my bride.

Do you remember our school play back in 1990? I had been chosen to play the fisherman, Daniel, who would row his wife, Rachel, across the river. It didn't matter that Daniel had only six words to speak – 'We will soon be there, dear'; it didn't matter that the boat was an upturned table with cardboard stuck to the sides and was pulled jerkingly across the stage by four stage hands who could all be seen by the entire audience; it didn't matter that the whole play lasted 25 minutes and Daniel was on the stage for less than one. What did matter was that Daniel was married to Rachel and that Rachel was played by you, Jayne. And today, Daniel has finally married Rachel for real.

Darling, thank you for making me the happiest man in the world. Someone once said, 'When you love someone, everything is clear – where to go, what to do – it all takes care of itself.' That's exactly how I feel today. When I asked a few of you earlier what Jayne looked like today, you all told me she looked wonderful, but this didn't prepare me for the sight I got when I turned round in the church to see for myself. You look gorgeous, darling. Marriage is our last, best chance to grow up. Today I grew up.

Propose a personalised toast on behalf of yourself and your bride to the bridesmaids and pageboys (unless your wife is going to speak and propose a toast to her attendants)

And finally, I must say a word of thanks to the delightful young ladies who have done such a great job in helping Jayne up the aisle today – although I hope she came to the church of her own free will. You all did your job magnificently. Obviously I will use you every time I get married from now on. Please join me in drinking a toast to Petunia, Iris, Primrose, Violet and Rose. Ladies and Gentlemen, I give you . . . the bridesmaids.

7 Making the Best Man's Speech

Your speech marks an important rite of passage for the groom. In the same way that the father of the bride's speech may symbolically signify both the end of the bride's existence as a single person and also a change in the most significant other person in her life, so a best man's speech may symbolically signify both the end of the groom's existence as a single person and also a change in the most significant other person in his life. In a sense you're handing over the baton to his new bride.

On a more superficial, yet equally important level, people simply want to sit back and have a good laugh at the groom's expense. And it's your job to make sure they are not disappointed. However, never say anything nasty, unpleasant or vindictive. Some good-natured mickey-taking is fine, but crossing the line into areas capable of causing real offence is easily done and must be avoided at all costs. The ideal speech will have them laughing at your verbal onslaught while, at the same time, thinking you really don't mean a word of it.

Getting the etiquette right

Traditionally, this would have been the third and final speech. However, as we have seen, other people, such as the bride, her mum or stepdad, may have also made their contribution to proceedings. So nowadays yours may not necessarily be the third speech. Yet however many other people may have spoken, it should still always be the *final* speech, the climax of the afternoon's or evening's words of wit and wisdom.

Officially, this is a response on behalf of all the attendants. Yet, in reality, its main purpose is to entertain the guests. Unlike the other two main speeches, its overall tone should not be too serious or emotional. Once you have thanked the bridegroom for his kind words, most of your speech should take the form of a humorous yet controlled verbal assault on him.

However, etiquette also demands that you need to say something more thoughtful, meaningful and complimentary about the bridegroom. This should be done towards the end of an otherwise upbeat and jokey speech. If the guests suddenly realise that you really do care about this man as a true and valued friend, they will be touched and you will have achieved the perfect response to any best man's speech: a marriage of cheers and tears.

To meet people's expectations, you may decide to include the following broad sections and messages.

- Hook your audience, introduce yourself and thank the bridegroom for the toast to the bridesmaids.

- Foreshadow the character attack which is to follow.

- Make a few general compliments.

- Roast the bridegroom.

- Compliment the bride.

- Congratulate the happy couple.

- Read any letters, cards, emails and texts that have been received.

- Praise the bridegroom, end on a high and propose a toast to the bride and bridegroom.

Some people argue that, strictly speaking, you should not toast the bride and groom because the father of the bride – and perhaps others – will have already done so. I disagree. After all, it's their day and a final toast to them makes a suitable climax to the speeches.

Making it unique and memorable

I don't want to be a spoilsport, but if you are going to prepare and present a brilliant speech you must stick to some ground rules. That does not mean you need to change from your trendy tuxedo into a straitjacket. Far from it. It simply means you are speaking at your friends' wedding reception, not at a stag do or funeral.

The best humour in a best man's speech will always have a personal resonance. There is no substitute for good, clean(ish) or even slightly risqué jokes and stories involving key members of the wedding party, particularly the bridegroom. Start early. Talk to the groom's friends, family and workmates, gathering stories and anecdotes about him. Which themes are emerging? Which stories are particularly funny or insightful? Which do your thoughts keep returning to, making you smile? Then hone in on one or two key ideas and make them the focus of your speech. Real-life stories are best. However, feel free to embellish them a little for emotional or comedic effect.

Choosing the right material

In any best man's speech there are safe, middling and dangerous subject areas. Here are some green, amber and red topics for you to consider. Green means safe as houses. Amber means they could be included, in moderation, if you know the audience is pretty broad-minded. Red means don't even think about it. As we are continually reminded, greens are good for you.

Green

- Childhood.
- School.
- College.
- Jobs.
- Hobbies.
- Characteristics.

- Friends.
- Ambitions.
- The perfect match.
- How they met.
- How you met.
- The venue (positive).
- The food (positive).
- Compliments.

Amber

- The stag do.
- The honeymoon.
- Mother-in-law jokes (if you are sure she and her partner won't be offended).

Red

- Exs.
- Anything iffy about the bride.
- Divorce.
- Unemployment.
- Addictions or counselling.
- Brushes with the law.
- Sexually transmitted diseases.
- Fetishes.
- Knocking marriage or weddings.
- Smutty jokes.
- Racist, sexist or homophobic jokes.
- The venue (negative).
- The food (negative).

Being creative

Try to be as original as you can. Use whatever material works for you. While true stories are unbeatable, there is nothing wrong with making a few little changes and revisions here and there to make them even funnier or more poignant. Also being original does *not* mean you shouldn't make use of other people's material. After all, *they* probably did. With a little thought and imagination an amusing story or one-liner can be adapted and personalised to suit your needs. No one minds – or even knows – if a good story is apocryphal, as long as it is witty and it sounds as if it *could* be true of the person about whom it is told.

If most of the guests know the groom is a tight-fisted so and so, you could say:

> [Groom's] *quite well off . . . but he never brags about it. In fact you could spend an entire evening with him down the pub and never know he's got a penny.*

However, there's no point in telling the most hilarious joke about his beer drinking exploits if his mates know his idea of a heavy night on the town is two pints of lager and a packet of cheese and onion crisps. All your caricatures must be based upon fundamental truths.

Sugaring your teasing remarks with praise

You also need to offer a few optimistic thoughts about the bride, the groom and the institution of marriage. Don't worry, you don't need to embarrass yourself and others by using gushing, extravagant language. A sincere compliment and a teasing jibe often fit well together. The trick is first to set up a situation which you can exploit with a teasing remark, before turning this into a genuine compliment. If the praise comes immediately after the crowd has had a good laugh, its effect on them will be at least doubled.

> *When I asked* [groom] *about the wedding arrangements* [set-up]*, he said, 'Oh, I'll leave all that to you. But I do want* Bells *– and at least three cases*

of it [tease].*' Well I don't know about Bells, but I work with* [groom] *at Waterloo Road Comprehensive – and I can tell you he's certainly one of the best* Teachers *I know* [praise].

Alternatively, you can build up the bridegroom with a public compliment, before bringing him down to earth with a bang. You simply reverse your tease and praise.

As you all know, [groom] *sells widgets for a living* [set-up]. *His boss says he is unquestionably the most independent salesman he has ever known* [praise] . . . *he doesn't take orders from anyone* [tease].

Gagging your gags?

When it comes to questions of taste and taboos, propriety and political correctness, ethics and etiquette, things continually change. You need to keep up with these changes and then use your own judgement and common sense, perhaps taking advice from the bride and groom.

The important thing to remember is that a wedding is a family occasion. And any speech which aims at the lowest common denominator will not inspire affection or respect, and such a performance is ultimately barren of any genuine humour. By all means choose something old, something new, something borrowed . . . but *never* anything blue.

The late and great comedian and public speaker Bob Monkhouse devised the following test for all his potential material. You can do the same, by asking yourself these questions.

1. Do *you* think it is funny?

2. Can you say it confidently and with comfort?

3. Is there any danger of offending anyone?

4. Will they understand and appreciate it?

Do you think it is funny?

If you are not really happy about a joke or story, you will not tell it well. Not only that, the guests probably won't find it funny either. Follow this showbiz adage: If in doubt, leave it out.

Can I say it confidently and with comfort?

Unless you are already an accomplished public speaker, avoid any material that requires a mastery of accents, immaculate timing, expressive gestures or practised articulation. It is far safer to choose more straightforward jokes and stories which allow you to relax and 'be yourself'.

Is there any danger of offending anyone?

Use your common sense on this one. Uncle Jack, in his electric wheelchair, would probably prefer to have his leg pulled about a fine he incurred for speeding to be at the wedding on time, than to be ignored altogether. However, don't ruin the bride's day by saying anything that undermines the institution of marriage or questions her morals.

Will they understand and appreciate it?

Your audience may be aged anything between 2 and 92 (nowadays even older) and they will probably have a wide range of backgrounds. So it is impossible to give a speech totally suited to everyone. However, what you can do is avoid extremes of, on the one hand, childish jokes and, on the other hand, telling complicated, technical stories, comprehensible only to a professor of nuclear physics.

Including some winning lines

The *best* best men always walk that fine line between irreverence and respect, ensuring that all their comments and observations are understood and appreciated by an audience which includes both children and the elderly. You are expected to include a humorous character assassination of the groom. However, it is important that insults and asides are seen to be good-natured. Smile as you turn the knife.

Here are some opening lines, jokes and one-liners, spoof messages and toasts, some of which you may wish to adapt and personalise for inclusion in your speech.

Opening lines

Ladies and Gentlemen, this is a truly historic day! This day, the 7th of October, will always be remembered because of three world-famous events. Captain Cook landed in New Zealand back in 1769, X Factor's Mr Nasty, Simon Cowell, was born in 1959, and on this day in 201X, you heard the finest best man's speech of your entire lifetime! Now ... who's going to make it? [Or some similar anniversary hook.]

Ladies and Gentlemen, I thought it was going to be difficult to follow Tim's speech ... and I was right ... I couldn't follow a damn word of it.

Ladies and Gentlemen, just once in a lifetime you get the opportunity to talk about a man blessed with dynamic charisma, devastating wit, stupendous talent and unstoppable personality ... but enough about me ... I'm going to be talking about Karl.

Ladies and Gentlemen, what can I say about Stu that hasn't already been said in open court?

Ladies and Gentlemen, I've been asked to say a few words, so here goes ... baboon ... socks ... cucumber [sit down, pause, then rise again]. *But the words I really want to share with you here today are about Danny ...*

Ladies and Gentlemen, it is not often that you get the chance to talk about a man bestowed with presence, personality and power ... a man who knows where he's going in life, and how he's going to get there ... but until that day comes along, I shall talk about Mark.

Fornication, fornication ... for-'n-occasion like this, it's an honour for me to be here, making this little speech. Ladies and Gentlemen ...

Ladies and Gentlemen, it's great to see so many familiar faces. Thank you so much for coming ... especially those who knew I was going to speak ... but who came anyway.

Ladies and Gentlemen, someone once said being asked to be the best man is like being asked to sleep with Camilla, Duchess of Cornwall ... it's a great honour to be asked, but nobody really wants to do it ...

Ladies and Gentlemen, I'm making this speech today under a considerable handicap – I'm sober.

Ladies and Gentlemen, not for the first time today, I rise nervously from a warm seat, with a piece of paper in my hand ...

Ladies and Gentlemen, first the good news: when I saw Patrick's new suit/shirt/tie this morning I was absolutely speechless ... Now the bad news: I've almost recovered from the shock, and the speech must go on.

Ladies and Gentlemen, when Ewan asked me to be his best man it came as quite a shock because I'd only known him for 18 months. But I guess you get close very quickly when you share a cell ...

Ladies and Gentlemen, the last time I stood up and addressed such well-dressed people, they gave me a £50 fine and a year's ASBO ... so I hope you're going to be kinder than that last lot ...

Ladies and Gentlemen, since we must always speak well of the dead, our only chance to knock them is while they're alive. So here goes ...

Ladies and Gentlemen, a wise man once said a best man's speech should last no longer than it takes the groom to make love ... so thank you and good evening [sit down].

Ladies and Gentlemen, my job today is to talk about Steven – and there are no skeletons in his cupboard – or so I thought ...

Jokes and one-liners

Every once in a while we have the opportunity to talk of a man of high achievement, transparent integrity and penetrating intellect. Not today though.

I've known Justin for 10 years now ... although my liver claims it's 50 ... and my wallet swears it's 100.

Jimmy made that speech for nothing and, I'm sure you'll agree, he was worth every penny.

When it came to writing this speech, I thought I'd get some ideas from the internet. After a couple of hours I found some really good stuff, but then I remembered I was writing a best man's speech.

I had to let my girlfriend down to be here today. Not to worry though, I can blow her back up again when I get home.

I'd like to sincerely thank Brandon for agreeing to be my groom today.

Isn't it funny how history repeats itself? Twenty-nine years ago, Maggie's mum and dad were sending their beautiful daughter to bed with a dummy – and here we are again today.

Eric, I'm really impressed with you ... I've never seen such a massive erection at a wedding before ... what a wonderful marquee you booked.

Cameron's always been a great friend to me...a real mate...he's special... at least that's what our school psychologist called him.

Kyle was born on 4 March 1983. His mum tells me he came prematurely... so nothing new there then, eh Amber?

Leroy was born back in 1976. Now I don't know if it's a coincidence or not, but a couple of weeks after he was born family planning was made available free on the National Health.

Nathan was a precocious child. He walked and talked before he was one; he could read and write before he was three; and he could forge his parents' signatures before he was five.

So what can I tell you about our groom? Well, he's cool, charming, caring, sophis?, sophistic? Sorry, Craig, your spelling is terrible. In fact, Craig's spelling is so awful that when he was younger, during his heavy metal devil worshipping stage, he once sold his soul to Santa.

Sean's an inoffensive sort of chap...but then again so was the Yorkshire Ripper.

Standing here today, I feel a real sense of panic... and the definition of the word 'panic' is when your partner, your rent and your library books are all a month overdue at the same time. That's not, of course, true of Jared, who took his books back last week...

I want to refute this vicious rumour that's been going around here today that the bride and groom had to get married. That's a wicked lie. They could easily have waited at least another fortnight.

Greg told me he's going to buy you all a drink – and a straw each so you can share it.

If I ever needed a brain transplant, I'd choose Corey's...because I'd want one that had never been used before.

Things never go right for Jagad ... if he went into the funeral business, people would stop dying.

There is absolutely nothing wrong with Tyler that a miracle can't fix.

Unusual name David Stiggers, so I looked it up. Apparently Stiggers is Old English for 'handsome, intelligent and generous'... David is Gaelic for 'not very'.

It only takes one drink to get Adam drunk – the fourteenth.

Antonio told me he bought his suit for a ridiculous figure. Looking at him today, I'm afraid I must agree.

Archie is so unlucky, if he were to be reincarnated, he'd probably come back as himself.

Brett was born on 18 January 1984. I tried to link it to some special world event but nothing much seemed to have happened on that day, although hospital staff still refer to it as Ugly Wednesday.

I think the world of him. Mind you, look at the state the world's in.

I suppose the time has come for me, too, to take a wife. The only question remains: Whose wife to take?

My ambition is to be the last man on earth – so that I can find out if all those girls were telling the truth.

Dustin's a man of rare gifts. He hasn't given one in years.

Tara finds Duggie very attractive. Then again, she is on heavy medication.

I have to say to you, that in all the years I have known him, no one has ever questioned his intelligence. In fact, I've never heard anyone mention it.

Since we met nearly ten years ago, there hasn't been a day when I haven't thought about him. And I haven't thought about him today either.

He was no oil painting when he was born ... in fact, his parents didn't know whether to buy a cot or a cage.

I was first introduced to Miguel at school by Hugh, our mutual friend who sadly could *be here today.*

The trouble with being best man at a wedding is that you never get the chance to prove it.

Noel is a man of hidden talents. I just hope some day he'll find them.

I'm sure the girl for me is just around the corner ... unless the police have moved her on since last night.

I asked Brandi what she wanted for a wedding present. She said a coffee percolator ... well actually she asked for a perky copulator ... but I knew what she meant.

You may have noticed how few single people were invited to the wedding. I will let you into a secret: that was Adrian's idea. He's very astute. He told me that if he invited only married people all the presents would be clear profit.

There's nothing I wouldn't do for Chad, and I know there's nothing he wouldn't do for me. In fact, we spend our lives doing nothing for each other.

When they eventually got round to talking about a little rumpy-pumpy, Megan said she wanted it infrequently ... Gordon replied: 'Is that one word or two?'

A man like Stan only comes along once in a lifetime – I'm only sorry it had to be during my *lifetime.*

There's no doubt about it, men have better taste than women. After all, Ricardo chose Christina – but Christina chose Ricardo.

None of you will know this, but I've actually congratulated the groom in private already. 'Ken,' I said, 'you will always look back on this day as the happiest and best thing you have ever done.' Fitting words, I thought, at the end of a fantastic stag weekend.

Erin, please place your right hand on the table and Joel, please place your left hand over Erin's hand [wait for them to do this]. *Joel, treasure this moment because you will never have the upper hand again.*

Spoof messages

Keep things interesting by providing a few background details about the people who sent messages (not just 'Uncle Tom' but 'Roy's 80-year-old Uncle Tom from South Africa, who decided to emigrate there on the day he first met Roy'). Try to save the most poignant or funny one until last. Alternatively, once you have read all the genuine ones, you could *make-up* the final message. If you do so, it must be obvious to everyone that it's a joke:

This last one comes from the girls at [her work, local, sports club, etc.]. *It says, 'There were three crucial stages to your ceremony today:*
The aisle – the longest walk you'll ever take
The altar – the place where two became one
The hymn – the choral celebration of marriage.'
Kristen, please repeat after me: 'Aisle, Altar, Hymn . . . Aisle, Altar, Hymn . . .'

And finally, here's one from that old quill-pusher, William Shakespeare. And it says, 'Sorry I can't be with you all today, but I'm Bard.' Shakey goes on: 'Now it hath been said that all unhappy marriages are a result of the husband having good looks and brains. Verily, therefore, I have total confidence that this marriage will be an exceptionally happy one.'

This last one is for Kelly and it comes from the lads at Wayne's soccer club: 'Congratulations, Kelly. We've tried Wayne in several different positions and he's useless in all of them . . . we wish you better luck.'

Here's the final message: 'Dear Dave and Sam, congratulations on your marriage. I trust that your recent purchases did the trick. Please can you come into the shop and settle your remaining bill as your credit limit has now been reached. Lot's of love for the future. Don't be strangers, signed Anne Summers' . . . Who is she?

This is the last one: 'To Richard, We'll miss the threesomes . . . Love, Ant and Dec.'

Oh, that's nice . . . even the caterers have sent you a message . . . it says: 'May your honeymoon be like a good Sunday roast: a bit of leg . . . a bit of breast . . . and lots of stuffing.'

These are the final couple of messages: 'To Miriam, We could have been so good together', Robbie Williams. To Nick, 'We could have been so good together', Robbie Williams.

And here's the last two messages: 'To Kevin, We could have been so good together', Cheryl Cole. To Fiona, 'We were so good together', Brad Pitt.

I don't know who these last people are. Do you know a Bob and Alice, Neil? Anyway, I'll read their message to the both of you: 'Congratulations on your wedding. Hope you are having a wonderful day. From Bob Farkin, Alice Farkin . . . and the whole Farkin family.'

Toasts

In the same way that your opening remarks should include both an attention-grabbing hook and a short response on behalf of the bridesmaids, so your final words (not literally, I trust) should include both a memorable closing line and a toast to the happy couple. Here are some possibilities, but, as always, try to be personal, relevant and original.

May the best day of your past be the worst day of your future. Ladies and Gentlemen – friends – please join me in a toast: The bride and groom.

May the roof above you never fall in, and may you never fall out.

Here's to her husband and here's to his wife,
May they be together for the rest of their life.

Down the hatch to a wonderful match.

I leave you with this thought . . . there are Seven Deadly Sins, enough for one each day. Have a great week's honeymoon. Ladies and Gentlemen, a toast: The bride and groom.

May all your ups and downs be under the duvet . . .

As I said to the woman I lost my virginity to, thanks for laughing. Ladies and Gentlemen, please raise you glasses. Let's drink a toast to . . .

A sample speech

So now it's time to put it all together. The main reason for providing this sample speech is to give you an idea of the sorts of things you should be saying and the style and tone you should adopt. You may wish to add a section, omit one, or perhaps combine two or more of them. That's up to you. My only advice is only make changes if you have a good reason to do so. Why reinvent the wheel? The following structure works.

Hook your audience, introduce yourself and thank the bridegroom for the toast to the bridesmaids

Ladies and Gentlemen, when Scott first asked me to be his best man, I told him that I was honoured, but I felt he'd be better off with someone else.

Then he offered me twenty quid. I was indignant . . . I'm not a man who can be bought. Then he upped his offer to fifty . . . Anyway, I'm Nick and it's a pleasure and privilege for me to be standing here before you today.

Now, as is customary at this stage, on behalf of the most delightful set of bridesmaids I have ever set my eyes on, I would like to thank Scott for his kind words and generous gifts. I'm not sure why they can't thank him themselves . . . but there we go. Girls, where did you learn to pout, look pretty and hold flowers all at the same time? I can't even look pretty when I'm not doing anything else.

And didn't the ushers do a great job, too? It's not easy being an usher. I was one at a mate's wedding recently and I asked a lady who was entering the church whether she was a friend of the groom. 'Most certainly not, young man,' she replied, 'I'm the bride's mother.'

Foreshadow the character attack which is to follow

Now my main job today is to tell you all about our dashing groom. So last night, while I sat on the couch putting this little speech together, I reviewed the high points of Scott's life . . . and I fell asleep.

Make a few general compliments

Well they've done it . . . they've finally tied the knot . . . they've married for better or for worse, which is quite appropriate because our groom couldn't have done any better . . . and our bride couldn't have done any worse. Scott, you are a very fortunate young man . . . you've married Sam, who is witty, intelligent and caring. She deserves a good husband. So thank your lucky stars you married her before she found one.

You know, I genuinely don't think things could have gone any better today. There are so many people to compliment and congratulate and I echo every word of thanks already spoken by Scott and Sam's dad, Mike.

And don't Sam and Scott look great, too? Come on . . . I'm sure you'll all agree . . . all those hours spent in the beauty parlour getting the hair, make-up and nails just right have really paid off . . . Scott, you look beautiful. No, seriously, Sam looks absolutely radiant . . . and Scott looks . . . well, like Scott.

Roast the bridegroom

So what can I tell you about a man who came from a humble background and is now rapidly rising to the top of his profession through sheer persistence, grit and willpower? A man of insight, humour and intelligence? A man who is beginning to distinguish himself in the cut-throat commercial world as a winner? Well that's enough about me . . . I'm here to talk about Scott.

Now I wanted to present a broad, balanced picture of our hero to you all here today. So over the last couple of weeks, I've been talking to lots of you to see what you think about him. When I heard words like 'ignorant', 'conceited' and 'lazy', I thought, hang on, that's a bit rough . . . but if his parents don't know him, who does?

I first met Scott when we were teenagers. My first impression of him was a guy with a really distinctive fashion sense. He always stood out from the crowd. Before too long, he became my role model and I started to copy the sorts of things he used to wear – until my mother grounded me for taking clothes from her wardrobe.

Scott was born just around the corner from here 32 years ago. He was so surprised by his birth that he was speechless for about a year and a half. Now I'm not saying he was an ugly baby, but his mum Mary used to put a bone around his neck, so the dog would play with him.

I asked his dad if he had any cute photos of Scott which I could show today. There was this really sweet one of him lying on a sheepskin rug playing with his little organ . . . he's always been a very musical chap . . . I was going to have it blown up to show you today, but then I thought it might be too embarrassing because it was only taken last year.

Shall I let you into a little secret? Shall I tell you about Scott's romantic proposal? Well, as most of you know, Sam and Scott met at Glastonbury Festival three years ago – the year it was boiling hot and really dry. They were camped right next to each other. Scott invited Sam in for a drink and, shall we say, the excitement that night was in-tents. Things moved on very quickly from there . . . perhaps a little more quickly than Scott had anticipated. Before too long they were having proper grown-up rows. A few months later, during a romantic dinner at the Bengal Spice, Scott knelt down to pick up a piece of chapatti he'd dropped . . . Sam jumped to conclusions and . . . well here we are all here today.

Compliment the bride

Sam, you look magnificent. Today really belongs to you and I am so proud to count you as a valued friend. You have the gift of finding joy everywhere and of leaving it behind when you go. If you had a pound for every smile you've put on a face, you'd be a millionaire. This morning Scott told me he loves you terribly. I replied, 'Don't worry, mate . . . with time and practice, you're sure to improve.'

Congratulate the happy couple

You know, you two guys are lucky people. Lucky to have found your best friend; lucky to be in love; lucky to know deep in your hearts that you're ready to share your lives together. And I know I speak for every person in the room when I wish you both a long and happy life together.

Read any letters, cards, emails and texts that have been received

Now, before I receive my standing ovation, it's time for me to read messages received from people who sadly couldn't be here with us here in person today . . .

[Read the genuine messages]

Ok, this is the last one and it comes from Sam's Great Aunty Florence from Florida: 'Sorry I can't be at the wedding, but please send me a photo of the bride . . . preferably mounted.' Whatever turns you on, Flo . . .

Praise the bridegroom, end on a high and propose a toast to the bride and bridegroom

So, in conclusion, how can I sum up Scott to you? A successful businessman? A talented dancer? A gifted footballer? Scott is in fact none of these. However, I'm sure he will be a brilliant husband.

You know, it's a rare opportunity to have such a public opportunity to tell your best mate how much you love him, and that is precisely what I say to you now. Scott, you are the friend everyone dreams of having. And, Sam, I know Scott will bring you as much happiness as a husband as he's brought to me as my best mate.

Ladies and Gentlemen, this wonderful day simply would not have been possible without the presence of the two most important people in this room. I think we should now raise our glasses to them, don't you? Ladies and Gentlemen, please be upstanding and join me in a final toast to two of the nicest people I know . . . to Sam and Scott.

8 Other Speeches

Until quite recently, tradition and etiquette demanded just three wedding speeches. However, in these days of varying family circumstances, it is possible, or even likely, that other people may also want or be asked to speak. Today it is not uncommon for the bride; her mother; a bridesmaid; one of the groom's parents; or a child, close friend or relative of the bride or groom to also say a few words. Fortunately, though, it is still rare for all of them to do so at the same wedding.

If any of these people are speaking *instead of* one of the 'big three', they would be expected to convey similar messages to the ones traditionally anticipated of those speakers (see Chapters 5 to 7). However, if they are modern optional *'additional'* speeches, there is no tradition and little etiquette to follow. And with no official toasts to make, they all have pretty much free rein in what they say, so long as their tone is positive and messages upbeat and congratulatory. That said, they may well wish to thank the bride and groom for asking or allowing them to say a few words – although a parent or child would not be expected to do this.

While it seems perfectly reasonable for a bride to share the speaking limelight with her husband and for a parent of the groom to have equal billing with the bride's dad, it is good manners for any other speakers to keep their contributions comparatively short and never to attempt to 'out-do' any of the traditional 'big three'.

Similarly, there is no traditional order of speeches to follow. If both parents of the bride wish to speak, perhaps they could make the first two speeches. However, if one or both parents of the groom also intend to say a few words, it might be better to alternate the speeches from bride-centred to groom-centred and back, in a kind of ping-pong fashion.

There is therefore much flexibility here and the order of speeches should reflect people's preferences and ultimately be what 'feels right'. The important thing is not only to ensure that anyone who wants to speak is allowed and indeed encouraged to do so, but also that each side of the family feels that their combined contributions are of roughly equal weight.

While not all wedding speech experts would agree, my advice would be to always keep the best man's speech till last. His is the long-established high spot of proceedings and it would be a shame if this traditional 'big finish' were to be lost.

Each of the following sample speeches ends with a toast. In practice, however, you may consider that half a dozen or more invitations to raise a glass is somewhat excessive. Some speakers may therefore decide instead to conclude with a simple but heartfelt expression of their good wishes for the future happiness of the newlyweds.

The bride's speech

The inclusion of a bride's speech is growing in popularity so rapidly that before too long we may be referring to the 'big four' rather than the 'big three'. It would be sensible for this speech to be made immediately after (or immediately before) your husband's. The two of you should decide in advance what topics and areas each will cover, to ensure that collectively you say everything you want to, and also that you avoid unnecessary duplication.

Here is a possible outline.

- Hook the audience.

- Thank your husband for marrying you (with an anecdote concerning the 'early days').

- Thank your parents for being so loving and supportive (possibly including a poignant or amusing childhood memory).

- Thank your in-laws for being so welcoming.

- Thank your attendants (possibly with a story of how you met and became friends).

- Propose a toast to the groom.

Alternatively, you may decide to propose a toast to your bridesmaids, instead of your husband (in both senses of the phrase).

A sample speech

Good afternoon, Ladies and Gentlemen, today I married my best friend, the one I laugh with, the one I live for, the one I love with every fibre of my soul. Hi, I'm Julie and, yes, I'm now going to break with tradition and say a few words of my own.

Well, I certainly don't want to repeat everything Keith has already said, but I must echo his sincere thanks to you all, both for your presence here and for your presents to us. We are so grateful. I also want to add just a few more personal thank yous of my own.

The first is simple and totally heartfelt: Keith, thank you for marrying me. You have made me the happiest woman in the world. Meeting you was like opening your first bottle of champagne; marrying you is like drinking it. You know, it only seems like yesterday that we were walking, hand-in-hand, along the Caribbean shoreline.

Actually, though, it was a year ago today. The sun was setting and there wasn't a sound to be heard except the rhythmical and relaxing splashing of the waves. As we strolled on, I could feel the cool warm sand rising between my toes. In the distance, fishing boats were returning with the day's catch. We had been together for three wonderful years, but this was our first romantic holiday together. And it was paradise.

As we walked on, I noticed lines in the sand at our feet, curving in and out and looping here and there. At first I thought nothing of it, but then it dawned on me that the line was forming letters. I looked forward and back, trying to work out what the words said . . . 'Will you . . .' Suddenly I knew; my mouth dropped open. Keith beamed from ear to ear and trotted forward, taking me with him towards the question mark further down the beach. A beautiful heart-shaped seashell was lying where the dot would have been. I picked it up. Something rattled inside. I shook it and this diamond ring fell into my hand.

Turning to Keith, I saw my husband-to-be looking up to me from bended knee, the question burning in his eyes. My acceptance was obvious and immediate as I ran to leap into his arms and embrace him with a kiss. Keith, that was the most romantic proposal a girl could ever receive. Within minutes the tide had swept away your words, but the memory of that magical moment will forever be etched upon my heart.

You know, memories are wonderful things and I could share a million others with you today. However, one childhood recollection always stands out in my mind. I was a bit of a tomboy and I loved nothing more than climbing trees. Dad had just moved in with mum and, to be honest, things were a bit awkward at home and I wasn't at all sure what to make of him.

One day the three of us were in the park when I got stuck in a massive oak tree. However hard I tried, I just couldn't get down. Dad said, 'Jump, I'll catch you.' 'What if you don't catch me?' I asked. 'I'll catch you. You must trust me.' Our eyes met and in a split second, both our different fears became one. 'Even I get scared at times,' dad said. 'Scared of what?' I asked. 'Right now I'm absolutely terrified that you don't trust me.' I smiled and, without further hesitation, jumped, landing safely in his strong outstretched arms. He looked down at me and with unspoken words, we both said, 'We don't need to be afraid anymore. We trust each other.' It was a momentous moment in both our lives.

Dad, you knew that the most important thing you could do for your children was to love their mother. Even though mum didn't live long enough to see this day, I one hundred per cent agree with everything you have said of her. Sue was the best mum in the world. She was really more like an elder sister than a mother. We were great friends, even through my Catherine Tate teenage years. How did you put up with me? Mum, I love you so much. And I know you would be as equally proud of Dad today as I am. Dad, you have been the perfect parent to me and I thank you for that with all my heart. How could I have ever doubted you? Dad, I love you, too.

But from today I am blessed with not just one, but three wonderful parents. Mavis and Dennis, thank you so much for welcoming me so warmly into your family – as we all now welcome you into ours. It's fantastic that from today our two families have been united into one.

Now before I hand over to Jimmy, I'd like to say a massive thanks to three great girls who I am proud to call best mates. I've known my bridesmaids, Charita, Lucy and Cheryl, since school . . . a wonderful time of dodgy hairdos, zits and constant arguments over whether to listen to the Spice Girls or Boyzone . . . both first time around. Girls, you have been great today – as always – the day simply wouldn't have been the same without you. We've been through so much together – both good and bad. And it means so much to me that you are all here today to share the best day of my life. Thank you so much.

Finally, I can't let an opportunity like this go by without proposing a toast to my fantastic husband: Being loved by you makes me feel protected but not smothered; challenged but not threatened; directed but not controlled; wanted but not possessed. You are the one with whom I am not afraid to become 'we'. Ladies and Gentlemen, please raise your glasses and join me in a toast to my wonderful husband . . . to Keith.

The mother of the bride's speech

The bride's mum may wish to expand upon her partner's thoughts by adding a few of her own, from a mother's point of view. If the bride's father has just offered some words of advice to the groom, why not offer some to your daughter? And if there's something special you want to say about your daughter and new son-in-law, this is the ideal time to say it. As with the bride and groom, you and your husband should co-ordinate your speeches to ensure collectively you say everything you want to – and you avoid unnecessary repetition.

Here is a possible structure.

- Hook the audience and introduce yourself.

- Talk about your daughter and your relationship with her.

- Share one or two childhood memories.

- Talk affectionately about the groom (and his family).

- Proffer some motherly advice.

- Wish them best wishes for the future and propose a toast.

If both mothers are going to speak, they could get together beforehand to plan a joke. Perhaps the first speaker could tell the groom that she doesn't want to be an interfering mother-in-law, so she will only visit them every day with a 'y' in it. Later on, the second mother could tell the bride that she appreciates that they will need their own space, so she will only visit them every day with a 'd' in it.

A sample speech

Good afternoon, everyone. It has been said that when children find true love, parents find true joy. Well, today Dan and I found true joy. Ladies and Gentlemen, for those of you who don't know me I'm Carol, Alice's mum, and I am delighted to have the chance to add just a few words of my own on this special day.

Quite simply, Alice is most sensitive and caring person I know. Last week she had to tell her class who'd been chosen for the school play ... and who hadn't. Tricky, you might think. Not so for Alice. Those who hadn't been given a part were told they'd been given the vital job of sitting in the audience and clapping and cheering wildly. Everyone was over the moon about the important jobs they had been given. Now that's what I call being diplomatic. Alice, I'm so proud of you and I want the world to know it. You have been the best daughter anyone could ever have asked for. You deserve such a perfect day as this.

You know, children are a great comfort to you in your old age. Mind you, they sometimes help you get there a bit faster, too. Today you are a considerate, polite, well-mannered young lady. But you weren't always like that, were you? I remember the day you came home from school and told us you'd been doing cartwheels all day because the boys had told you you were so good at them. I said, 'Alice, they only want you to do cartwheels so they can see your knickers.' And you replied, 'I know that, Mum. That's why I took them off first.' Fortunately, you've acquired a little more finesse since then.

And what about this debonair young man at your side? Ben, Dan and I are so impressed with you. You've proved yourself to be a hard-working, dependable and trustworthy person with absolutely immaculate tastes. After all, you support United and you chose Alice, didn't you? Ben, we are both absolutely delighted that you have married our darling daughter. You deserve each other. And on that note, I'd like to propose a little toast to you: Here's to the groom ... a man who has won not only the bride's heart, but also her mother's.

Now before I sit down, I'd like to pass on a little advice to my daughter and her new hubbie that has served Dan and me well over the years. So here goes. Happiness in marriage is not something that just happens. A good marriage has to be created. Always remember that in marriage the little things are the big things. It is never being too old to hold hands. It is remembering to say, 'I love you' at least once a day. It is never taking each other for granted; the romance shouldn't end with the honeymoon, it should continue through all the years. At times it won't be easy but, believe me, it will be so worth it when you look into your partner's eyes at your child's wedding – as I look into Dan's today – and you say, 'I still do.'

But today the day really belongs to Alice and Ben and I think we should now drink a toast to them, don't you? Everyone who knows them is certain that this is a marriage made in heaven, and I know that you will all want to join me in wishing them a long and happy married life together. Ladies and Gentlemen, please stand and make sure your glasses are fully charged – mine is being charged to Mastercard. Please raise your glasses and drink to the health and happiness of Alice and Ben.

To Alice and Ben.

The mother or father of the groom's speech

Whether it's the groom's mum or his dad who is going to speak, the messages they convey are likely to be the same. Essentially, you will probably want to take the opportunity to say how much the marriage means to you and to warmly welcome the bride into your family.

Here is a possible structure.

- Hook the audience and introduce yourself.

- Talk positively about the bride's parents, thanking them for laying on the reception – if they have.

- Talk affectionately about your son. Tell him how much he means to you.

- Welcome his bride into your family.

- Talk about the bride and the effect she has had on your son.

- Wish them all the best for the future and propose a toast.

The groom's father could also pay compliments to all the women and girls in the wedding party before concluding his speech with a toast to 'the ladies'. However, he may prefer use the opportunity to talk affectionately about his son.

A sample speech

Ladies and Gentlemen, we are told that marriage is a lottery. Well if it is, then these two certainly have hit the jackpot. They are both wonderful people who were meant for each other. Hello, everyone. For those of you who don't know me, I'm Cliff, Martin's dad, and it is my privilege to be speaking to you all here this afternoon.

Well I'm sure you'll all agree that things could not have gone better, so I'd like to take this opportunity to thank everyone who has been involved in all the planning and financing of today's fun and festivities. In particular, I'd like to thank Suzie's parents, Pat and Bill, for all their help and generosity.

You know, today is a celebration, but not just of the love that has united Martin and Suzie in holy matrimony, but also of the families that have created, moulded and influenced the lives of these two special people. So Ruth and I would also love to take this opportunity to publicly extend a hand of love and friendship to Pat and Bill – and all their family and friends.

Bill, it was wonderful to hear such lovely stories about Suzie's childhood. Well, Martin has been a fantastic son to us, too, and he's provided my wife and me with 20 years of uninterrupted happiness. I know he's 25, but for the first five years of his life he was a right little nightmare.

Oh yes, I have so many wonderful memories of Martin. Ruth will probably recall that infamous day when Martin was really playing up. His mum told him to behave himself. 'I will for a fiver,' Martin replied. And his mother said, 'Martin, you should be good for nothing, just like your father.' Then there was the time I had a terrible throat. I couldn't eat, drink or even talk. When the doctor called, Martin said to him: 'Dad's got a drinking problem. What can you do to help him?'

Martin has always been a very special son – kind, considerate, loving – a source of great pride and joy as Ruth and I watched him grow. We shared his birth cries and smiled though his first steps, his first words, his first giggles. We beamed through school concerts, sports days and birthdays. We shared laughter and tears. Every passing year gave us events to remember and memories to cherish.

Martin, we are proud to call ourselves your parents. No parents could hope for a bitter son . . . sorry, a better son. Martin, your handwriting is atrocious. No, seriously, these really are my own words and feelings. Mum and I are so proud of you.

Suzie, you've married a genius in the art of living and in the art of life. Mind you, Martin has married an absolutely wonderful woman, too. As we've got to know you well over the last year or so, Ruth and I have come to inescapable conclusion that – quite simply – Martin could not have done better. Suzie, you have shown yourself to be exactly the sort of person we had hoped Martin would marry: a dependable, loving girl with a great sense of humour. Suzie, it is a real honour and privilege for Ruth and me to formally welcome you into our family.

You have managed to transform our night owl into a homing pigeon. I've heard it said that love is born with the pleasure of looking at each other . . . it is fed with the necessity of seeing each other . . . it is concluded with the impossibility of separation. You two are inseparable. Martin has not only found someone he can live with, he has found someone he can't live without – and I wish you both love, health and eternal happiness. Ladies and Gentlemen, I give you the love birds: the bride and groom.

The bridesmaid's speech

The chief bridesmaid or maid of honour may wish to talk affectionately about the bride and their relationship. Or she may wish to have a little fun at her friend's expense. As with the best man's speech, the most effective bridesmaids' speeches will contain a balanced combination of both sincerity and humour.

Here is a possible structure.

- Hook the audience and introduce yourself.

- Thank the bride and groom for inviting you to speak.

- Give a humorous description of your relationship with the bride.

- Describe her as a person, combining sincerity with humour.

- Tell an amusing story about bride and/or the couple.

- Offer some humorous advice about relationships or marriage.

- Turn more serious. Tell her what she means to you.

- Wish them all the best for the future and propose a toast.

You will also need to decide whether you or the best man will respond to the groom's (or bride's) toast to the bridesmaids and the order of speeches will be largely dictated by this decision. Basically, whoever responds should speak immediately after whoever proposes the toast. However, it is recommended that the best man should *always* be the day's final speaker.

A sample speech

Can everyone hear me at the back? Yeah. Okay, mine's a large Chardonnay. Good afternoon, Ladies and Gentlemen, Boys and Girls. For those of you who don't know me – and for those who don't recognise me out of my jodhpurs and riding hat – my name is Jasmine, Sarah's chief bridesmaid. I'm very grateful to her for asking me to support her in this role today and to Robbie and her for giving me the additional honour of saying a few words of my own.

Now I've known Sarah since secondary school and I suppose it was inevitable that we would become good friends considering our mutual love no...not you, Robbie...horses. Yes, we've always enjoyed a stable relationship. My first horse was called Fly and Sarah's was Radish. We used to go round telling everyone that this was my horse Fly and her horse Radish.

Sarah's a great kid...my best friend. And I was so proud today to see her as she swept down the aisle. Proud and surprised...I shared a flat with her for two years and I've never seen her sweep anything before. But seriously, no one could have asked more from a friend. You have always been there when I've needed you. You deserve happiness and with Robbie I am confident you have found it. It's really great to see you two getting it together today...as it were.

I could share so many stories with you about Sarah. Let's just say she can be a little dippy. On her last birthday...no, I'm not telling you her age...Robbie took her shopping for her present. They saw a lovely bra and knickers set in M&S. Sarah stopped to look at them for a second and then, grabbing her boyfriend's hand, asked, 'Do you think I'd look good in those?' With a broad Brummie accent he replied, 'I don't know. Why don't you ask your boyfriend?' Instead of grabbing Robbie's hand she had grabbed someone else's and – even worse – the guy's girlfriend was holding his other hand. Nice one, Sarah. I'm not quite sure how that story ends, but Robbie tells me the four of you are now the best of friends!

Now how can Sarah and Robbie ensure a happy marriage? I know they've already had loads of advice that has been handed down from generation to generation...and no doubt been ignored by all of them. That's because most of this advice is given by men ... and to men. What do they know? Well, I'm a woman and I can tell you like it really is. It's all about communication. Robbie, here's a quick lesson on female speak which you would be wise to reflect upon...

When Sarah uses the word 'Nothing', she actually means 'something' ...you know: 'What's wrong, love?'... 'Oh, nothing'.

...and when she says, 'Go ahead', this means, 'Do it if you want...I don't really want you to...but I've lost interest'.

...and when she says, 'Fine', this really means, 'Look, I'm right...and your best bet is to shut up.'

So Robbie, if you hear Sarah say 'nothing', 'go ahead' and 'fine' within a couple of minutes of each other, be on your guard...but remember you, too, have a few words to fall back on... 'yes'... 'dear'... 'buy it'.

I hope that clears up any misunderstandings...

And now a little advice for my best friend: Sarah, if you think the way to a man's heart is through his stomach, you're aiming too high.

Winding up, in all sincerity, I'd like to say you two are great people and I'm proud to count myself as one of your friends. And without wishing to get all soppy, I want to tell you both here and now how much I love you...in a platonic sort of way, Robbie...before you get any ideas...and I wish you both the very best for your future together...you both deserve it. Ladies and Gentlemen, please join me in a toast to two great people: the bride and groom.

The son or daughter of the bride or groom's speech

No one should be pressurised into speaking at a wedding. Sweet as it may sound to hear the innocent, perhaps naïve words of a young child, it would be grossly unfair – even abusive – to *expect* a youngster to talk in front of a room of adults, many of whom they may not even know. That said, if anyone genuinely *wants* to say a few words, they should be encouraged to do so. And in the case of younger children, it may be literally the case of a few words. For a child to say, 'I'm very happy' is really saying everything we need to know.

Of course, an older child, possibly in his or her teens, may well wish to develop this thought. As always, precisely what you say depends upon so many factors and this is but one possible structure.

- Introduce yourself.

- Say how happy you are – and why.

- Wish them all the best for the future and propose a toast.

- Children of parents (re-)marrying later in life, may wish to add some of the sections and messages considered appropriate for a close family friend or relative, although the emotion they convey may be even stronger.

A sample speech

Hello everyone, I'm Chelsea, Tim's daughter, and I would like to say a few words to you all.

I know I speak for everyone here when I say congratulations to Tim and Lucy. I have never seen my dad as happy as he looks today and that makes me happy, too. Mum died five years ago and of course we still miss her terribly. In a sense she always will be part of our family. But deep down I knew – and hoped – that one day dad would meet someone else to share his life with and I'm absolutely delighted that now he has.

Lucy, you have had some effect on him. Look, he's even cut his hair. I know you'd never try to replace my mum – no one ever could – but we have a fantastic relationship that gets stronger every day, don't we?

It's great that you guys got married today and I wish you both all the very best for the future. Now I'm not really allowed to drink but I'm sure a little sip won't hurt. So please join me in a toast to two wonderful people ... Ladies and Gentlemen: to Tim and Lucy.

The close friend or relative's speech

Sometimes a person with a particularly special relationship with one or both of the couple may wish, or may be asked to make a speech. Don't hold back in saying precisely what you feel about them and consequently what this day means to you.

Here is a possible structure.

- Introduce yourself and explain your relationship with the bride, the groom or the couple.

- Thank them for inviting you to speak.

- Say what she/he/they mean(s) to you and how important this day is.

- Share a poignant memory or a funny story.

- Talk about her/his new spouse and how they seem together.

- Offer some light-hearted marital advice.

- Wish them all the best for the future and propose a toast.

The key to getting this speech right is to remember that your words are intended to give the audience your unique take on the person(s) you are speaking of.

A sample speech

Good afternoon, everyone. For those of you who don't know me, I'm John, Abigail's next-door neighbour, and Abbie and Francis have done me the great honour of offering me the opportunity of saying a few words on this joyous occasion.

Now I first got to know Abbie and her parents many years ago. It was back in 1990 when Henry, Catherine and a young Abbie came to live next door. Even in those days I found it a little difficult to get around but it wasn't too long before Abbie was not only doing errands for me, but she was also pushing me around in my wheelchair. So I simply had to be here today to say thank you and to wish you all the best for the future.

Your dad, Henry, was an excellent gardener and he soon transformed not only his garden, but mine as well. In fact we were in my greenhouse when he told me you had met Francis. He spoke very highly of the young man on that June evening and on many subsequent occasions. Although we all greatly miss Henry, we can rejoice in the fact that he would have been absolutely delighted that Francis and Abbie have become man and wife. And because his hopes and wishes have now been realised, I feel that in a sense he is celebrating here with us today. Catherine, you were married to a wonderful man, my best friend.

As you know, the wedding had to be postponed, but Abbie is a girl worth waiting for. Doesn't she look radiant? Henry would have been so proud of you . . . as I am sure Francis and Catherine are. I have got to know Francis very well since we first met last summer and I know Abbie has made an incredibly wise choice. He's a hard-working lad who knows where he's going in life . . . and how he's going to get there. These two young people were meant for one another and I'm certain they will share a wonderfully bright future together.

Now I had a little chat with Abbie this morning about marriage and how her life is going to change. I spoke about the hours of ironing, cooking and washing up . . . and Francis, I am delighted to tell you that for the first couple of months Abbie has agreed to help you out.

Well, as I said, I simply couldn't let the wedding of the nicest, kindest girl in the world go by without being here and putting on the record how much you mean to me and how proud Henry would have been of you today. You're simply the best.

I'll offer just one final thought: May we all live to be present at their golden wedding. Ladies and Gentlemen, I give you . . . the bride and groom.

Resources

The following lists provide a selection of other books and some websites where you may find further useful information relevant to preparing and delivering your speech.

Wedding etiquette

Wedding Etiquette, Patricia and William Derraugh (Foulsham, 1998).
Wedding Etiquette, Libby Norman (New Holland, 2007).
Wedding Etiquette, Antonia Swinson (Ryland Peters and Small, 2010).

www.countybride.co.uk
www.frugalbride.com
www.toastmaster4u.com

The main players

The Bride's Book, Carole Hamilton (Foulsham, 2007).
A Modern Girl's Guide to Getting Hitched, Sarah Ivens (Piatkus, 2002).
Making the Bridegroom's Speech, John Bowden (How To Books, 2000).
The Best Man's Handbook, Henry Russell (David and Charles, 1990).
Making the Best Man's Speech, John Bowden (How To Books, 2000).
The Complete Best Man, John Bowden (How To Books, 2006).
Father of the Bride: Speech and Duties, John Bowden (How To Books, 2010).
Making the Father of the Bride's Speech, John Bowden (How To Books, 2000).
How to be a Bridesmaid, Amy Elliot (Ryland Peters and Small, 2007).

www.confetti.co.uk

www.hitched.co.uk

www.weddingguide.co.uk

Second marriages

How to Get Married Again, Jill Curtis (Hodder and Stoughton, 2003).

www.idotaketwo.com

Public speaking

Mitch Murray's Handbook for the Terrified Speaker, (Foulsham, 1999).

Just Say A Few Words, Bob Monkhouse (Virgin Books, 2004).

High Impact Speeches, Richard Heller (Prentice Hall, 2002).

Lend Me Your Ears, Max Atkinson (Vermilion, 2004).

Speaking in Public, John Bowden (How To Books, 1999).

www.publicspeakingexpert.co.uk

Anniversaries

Pocket On This Day, David Crystal (Penguin, 2006).

Chambers' Dates, G.L. Hough, Editor (Chambers, 1989).

On This Day: Over 2000 Years of Front-Page History, Sian Facer, Editor (Gramercy Books, 2005).

www.bbc.co.uk/onthisday

Quotations

The library shelves are weighed down with these books. I find the following particularly useful:

The Funniest Thing You Ever Said, Rosemarie Jarski (Embury Press, 2010).

The Oxford Book of Quotations, Elizabeth Knowles, Editor (OUP, 2009).

The Penguin Dictionary of Humorous Quotations, Fred Metcalf (Penguin, 1987).

The New Penguin Dictionary of Quotations, Robert Andrews (Penguin, 2006).

A Dictionary of Twentieth Century Quotations, Nigel Rees (Fontana, 1987).

The Guinness Dictionary of Quotations for all Occasions, Gareth Sharpe (Guinness Publishing, 1994).

www.love-quotes-and-quotations.com

www.quotationspage.com

Anecdotes and jokes

There are hundreds – perhaps thousands – of these books. Here is a personal selection.

One Liners for Weddings, Mitch Murray (Foulsham, 2008).

Harry Hill's Whopping Great Joke Book, Harry Hill (Faber and Faber, 2010).

Biggest Ever Tim Vine Joke Book, Tim Vine (Century, 2010).

'Nuts' Joke Book, Nuts Magazine (Carlton Books, 2006).

The Naked Jape, Jimmy Carr and Lucy Greeves (Penguin, 2007).

There are numerous websites where you will find wedding and marriage-related jokes and stories which can be adapted and personalised for your speech. However, many of these sites seem to simply copy and paste material from one another. Do a search for 'wedding jokes', 'marriage jokes' and so on.

Miscellaneous

Relaxation and Stress Reduction Workbook, Martha Davis and Elizabeth Robbins Ashelman (New Harbinger, 2008).

The Power of Your Subconscious Mind, Joseph Murphy (Pocket Books, 2008).

Creative Visualization, Shakti Gawain (New World Library, 2002).

Use Your Head, Tony Buzan (BBC Active, 2006).

Voice and the Actor, Peter Brook and Cicely Berry (Harrap, 2000).
The Definitive Book of Body Language, Allan and Barbara Pease (Orion, 2005).

www.relaxation.com
www.mindtools.com

Index

order of speeches, usual, 1, 5–6, 66, 87, 100, 120–1, 130
originality, importance of (*see also* selecting), 20–1, 48, 62–5

pace, your, 50
pausing, importance of, 34, 50–1
personalising material, 6, 21, 104, 107
positive thinking, importance of, 39
posture, appropriate, 52
purpose, knowing your, 2–3

quotation close, the, 28
quotation hook, the, 14, 15–16, 28–9

rehearsing, 9, 38, 46–65
relative's speech, 134–5
relevance, ensuring, 11, 20–1
relaxation, (*see also* confidence; nerves; subconscious), importance of, 38
techniques, 41–4

script, 34–7, 57
cue cards, 35, 57
drafts, 34
outline, 34

second (and subsequent) marriages, 8
selecting material, *see* Monkhouse (*see also* adapting; humour; offensiveness; originality, personalising; relevance; sincerity; subconscious), 8, 20–1, 69, 102–3
sentimental close, the, 29
seriousness, when appropriate?, 6
shock close, the, 30
sincerity, essentialness of, 6, 10–11
speaking skills, *see* voice
stance, *see* posture
step-parent's speech, 1, 7, 11
subconscious mind, tapping the immense power of your, 39–40, 69

text, 35–6
themes, common, in all successful speeches, 10–11, 19–28, 47–8, 69
toastmaster, 1–2, 4, 6
toasts (*see also* order), 2–5, 9, 28–9, 31, 77–9, 94–5, 101, 114, 121

visualising success (*see also* positive thinking), 38, 40, 42–4
voice skills, developing your, 48–53

winning lines, 106
wit and wisdom close, the, 30–1

Some other titles from How To Books

THE DIY WEDDING MANUAL
How to create your perfect day without a celebrity budget
LISA SODEAU

This book will show you that with a little bit of planning and preparation, it is possible to have the day of your dreams without starting married life in debt. It's packed with money-saving ideas for: stationery, flowers, transport, hair and make-up, photographs, food and drink, the reception and much more – including tips from real brides and over 100 budget busting ideas.

ISBN 978-1-84528-405-3

THE STEP-BY-STEP GUIDE TO PLANNING YOUR WEDDING
LYNDA WRIGHT

Your wedding day marks the beginning of a new and exciting chapter in your life, so you'll want to make sure it's as wonderful as you always dreamed it would be.

This book will guide you through all the organisational detail of your wedding preparations so that you'll feel completely confident about the many choices and decisions you will have to make. It concentrates on the practical aspects of preparing for your big day and includes a countdown calendar, action plans, and checklists.

ISBN 978-1-84528-410-7

PLANNING A WEDDING
ELIZABETH CATHERINE MYERS

This book contains everything you need to know to plan a wedding. With it you will feel confident that you have all the details covered, and that everything is in place for a successful and happy day.

Ideas, checklists, tips and reminders will help make sure that you cover all the areas you need to, including the ones that are easy to miss. And you will be able to keep everything you need in one place.

'Full of essential information, tips and ideas, and the handy task list will help make sure the preparation goes without a hitch.' *Wedding Cakes*

ISBN 978-1-84528-389-6

FATHER OF THE BRIDE: SPEECH AND DUTIES
JOHN BOWDEN

As father-of-the-bride this will be a big day for you, too, with the speech playing an important part in the proceedings. You'll want to get it just right so that you speak from the heart but enliven sentiment with humour, and your speech is remembered for years to come – for all the right reasons. This book is packed with valuable tips and advice about conveying just the right messages to your daughter and her husband-to-be, understanding what is traditionally expected of you and making a memorable speech.

ISBN 978-1-84528-400-8

MAKING THE BEST MAN'S SPEECH
JOHN BOWDEN

'You can be funny, entertaining and good value for your best mate. . . .'

So you've been asked to 'say a few words' on the big day. The problem is that we don't get much practice do we? That's why this little handbook will prove so useful to you. Quite simply, it will show you how to prepare and present a unique and memorable best man's speech that even the most seasoned public speaker would be proud of.

- Includes jokes, ideas and sample speeches
- How to make them laugh
- Making fear your friend
- Dealing with the formalities
- Remembering the golden rules

'My speech went down a storm, because it was written from the heart following the simple guidelines within this excellent and very accessible book.' *Reader review*

John Bowden has over 20 years' experience as a professional trainer and senior lecturer in communication skills. He has written several books on speech making and is a member of the Comedy Writers' Association.

ISBN 978-1-85703-659-6

MAKING THE BRIDEGROOM'S SPEECH
JOHN BOWDEN
'Written specially and exclusively for the trepidatious bridegroom.'

As the bridegroom you are expected to say a few words on your big day. You'd rather run a marathon than give a speech? Don't panic – help is at hand. This handy guide provides you with all the tools you'll need to make a brilliant, memorable speech. The author, a professional speaker, reveals how to:

- Prepare your script
- Find the right tone
- Start and finish in style
- Deliver your speech with confidence
- Thank everyone involved

And to make it easier for you he has included plenty of ideas, quotations, one-liners and sample speeches

'After a couple of hours reading this entertaining and helpful book, I was ready to start putting my speech together with confidence and optimism that I didn't have before. Well worth the money.' *Reader review*

ISBN 978-1-85703-567-4

MAKING THE FATHER OF THE BRIDE'S SPEECH
JOHN BOWDEN
'Helps you open your heart and show your feelings.'

Your daughter is getting married and you have to make a speech. Don't be stuck for words on her special day! This practical book reveals all you need to know to make a speech which is both meaningful and joyous. The author, a professional speaker, shares his tricks of the trade:

- Ideas, quotations, one-liners and sample speeches
- Preparation and presentation
- Beginning and ending in style
- What to say and what to leave out
- Coping with nerves

With this book you can help make your daughter's special day thoroughly memorable – and enjoy it yourself too!

ISBN 978-1-85703-568-1

How To Books are available through all good bookshops, or you can order direct from us through Grantham Book Services.

Tel: +44 (0)1476 541080
Fax: +44 (0)1476 541061
Email: *orders@gbs.tbs-ltd.co.uk*

Or via our website
www.howtobooks.co.uk

To order via any of these methods please quote the title(s) of the book(s) and your credit card number together with its expiry date.

For further information about our books and catalogue, please contact:

How To Books
Spring Hill House,
Spring Hill Road,
Begbroke
Oxford OX5 1RX,

Visit our web site at

www.howtobooks.co.uk

Or you can contact us by email at *info@howtobooks.co.uk*